# The Dow Jones Index for Intellectual Sphere

# The Dow Jones Index for Intellectual Sphere

Sergey Khrystenko

iUniverse, Inc.

New York  Lincoln  Shanghai

# The Dow Jones Index for Intellectual Sphere

iUniverse books may be ordered through booksellers or by contacting:

iUniverse
2021 Pine Lake Road, Suite 100
Lincoln, NE 68512
www.iuniverse.com
1-800-Authors (1-800-288-4677)

Because of the dynamic nature of the Internet, any Web addresses or links contained in this book may have changed since publication and may no longer be valid.

The information, ideas, and suggestions in this book are not intended to render professional advice. Before following any suggestions contained in this book, you should consult your personal accountant or other financial advisor. Neither the author nor the publisher shall be liable or responsible for any loss or damage allegedly arising as a consequence of your use or application of any information or suggestions in this book.

ISBN: 978-0-595-44127-3 (pbk)
ISBN: 978-0-595-88451-3 (ebk)

Printed in the United States of America

# Contents

**PART 3**

**THE UNESCO STOCK EXCHANGE INDEX**

**PART 4**

**THE REPRODUCTION OF THE INTELLECTUAL SPHERE**

# Synopsis

The analysis of the economic parameters of the Intellectual Sphere in the USA, European countries and Japan, shows that this sector came close to the economic parameters of the Material Sphere.

In the Intellectual Sphere, millions of people and billions of US dollars are involved. Is the index for the Intellectual Sphere is absent to this day?

The absence of the exchange index in the Intellectual Sphere of the USA and other economically developed countries has a negative effect on everything. It is difficult to talk definitely about the tendencies on the market of informational and entertainment services.

Today, it is imperative that we create the stock exchange index for the Intellectual Sphere which would resemble that of the Dow-Jones index. But, for the exchange index of the Intellectual Sphere, I suggest using another logic that differs from that logic used in 1897.

Firstly, at creating the stock exchange index (SEI) of the intellectual sphere, I proceed from the fact that the intellectual sphere represents the economic system, the resources of which are moving in economic space.

Secondary, indexes should be of two kinds for intellectual values and intellectual services.

Thirdly, at creating SEI of the intellectual sphere I suggest taking into account complex numbers.

# Introduction

In 1997, the 100-year anniversary of Dow-Jones index was widely celebrated. It is still used in not only by businessmen, stock brokers, speculators of securities, but also by representatives of various economic schools. But is everything perfect in this index?

Many specialists say that it does not have any shortcomings. To confirm this, I suggest checking the logic behind Dow-Jones' index.

Nowadays, this index is used by 30 industrial, 20 transportation and 15 municipal companies. Let us examine it in a 3-dimensional space:

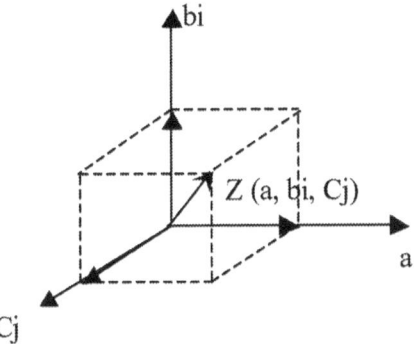

Where:

a—the vector of the enterprise securities of the material sphere

bi—the vector of the enterprise securities of the transportation sphere

Cj—the vector of the municipal enterprise securities

Index «DJ» = a + bi + Cj

At first glance at the 3-dimensional index, we do not find any internal logical defects. On the outside, it seems presentable and on the inside, convincing. It is, in fact, voluminous and, if you want, «starched», and so on.

Today, we do not have to change the internal logic of Dow-Jones' index, but only the increase of the quantity of the companies in each group of securities.

  - Dow-Jones' index—100 companies of the material sphere

  - Dow-Jones' index—100 companies of the transportation sphere

  - Dow-Jones' index—100 companies of the municipal sphere


But in this case, problems arise concerning the definition of the proportions between the a, b, C vectors. Such an approach in this sphere of exchanging indexes puts off the solutions to the problems to the far future.

The problem with Dow-Jones' index («DJ») can be examined with scrutiny.

We have to admit that the index has some minor deficiencies of not only logical, but psychological character.

There is a psychological barrier that we do not see but we are hinted on the fact that we do not have the right and conscience to criticize the «DJ» index. It is up to us to surpass all of this. If we were to speak about conscience, then we have to roll up the parameters of this category, but only in the limits of Dow-Jones' problems.

Law problems in economic achievements exist. But we should not ask anyone for the permission to examine the problems of this, or some other index.

  1.  Today, the users of the «DJ» index do not understand that it does not have the quality fulfillment it did a hundred years ago. For the past few years, the Dow-Jones index has been resembled an old wheel that is bouncing on humps and is letting out a part of its 100-year old pumped air. The reader cannot fully evaluate independently this situation. For a hundred years, the services sector increased by fifteen times from 5% to 76% in the GDP. Yes, today in the States, services consist of 76% of the GDP. In this relation, the Dow-Jones index should to consist of 76% of the values of service enterprises and of 24% of industrial enterprises. This proportion should be upheld in the conditions that you are planning to use the criteria in maximum but not partial adequacy.

  2.  Nowadays, the objectively used structure of the GDP does not attributes to the logic and contours of not only the Dow-Jones index but other

similar indexes. Today in the logical structure of the «DJ» index, obsolete logic is used.

-   First of all, in some cases, the value of the shares is defined by expenses. This relates to, firstly, the economic service branch where not all used resources are included in service values.

-   Secondly, in its structure, there are no company shares that create intellectual services—educational, enlightenment and entertainment.

-   Thirdly, it does not include the exchange index in medical services.

Today, the logic of the Dow-Jones index, has lost its topicality because it almost does not reflect the situation on the service market.

The «DJ» index does not point out anything on the economic service branches. Here, we remember pertinently the exchange joke that relates to this situation. «There is Dow but no Jones».

Can we use the «DJ» index without the supplementary and logical corrections?

Firstly, we should not act as «Headless Horsemen» who gallop on a great service field, not specifying the structure of the non-material market and not knowing the tendencies of the market—which services there improve and which deteriorate.

Secondly, we cannot use the Dow-Jones index anymore. The time has come to reconsider the logical structure of the Dow-Jones index. This should have been done a long time ago.

Thirdly, here we should calm down the stock brokers and businessmen that the falling down of the stock price of the shares in the industrial sphere is not the basis of worrying. In American and European economics, the service segment of the market is very advanced. But, the only deficiency lies in the lack of high-grade indexes of service market securities.

# PART 1

## THE DOUBLE ACCOUNTANCY RESOURCES IN THE INTELLECTUAL SPHERE

In 1932 a manual entitled "Accounting" for College and University Students was published—this manual is re-published, without any changes, every two or three years. This constant can be evaluated positively, but only for the material sphere branches.

This constant can be evaluated negatively. In 80 years in the theory of accounting, nothing has changed in the branches of production services. This theory has not been subjected to neither wars, revolutions, famine, nor cold.

What surprises me is that the accounting which is used in the material sphere is being "put on" the intellectual sphere without taking into account its specifics.

You be to judge.

The economic theories of the intellectual sphere are not developed. In the theory of enlightenment, education and entertainment we are missing chapter and books where the problems of the classification, expenses and results would be examined, there are no chapters concerning the accounting of the spare time of the population resources. Today, we are missing criteria of the intellectual welfare of the population. Today two bookshelves are missing on the economics of the intellectual sphere.

The accounting of the resources of the intellectual sphere bring about irritation: traditional resources are counted, whereas non-traditional ones (eg. The spare time of the population) are not.

In economic theories, the working time of the population is thought to be a traditional economic resources, on one hand. On the other hand, though, the spare time is not considered to be an economic resource. This paradox has existed for hundreds of years. Today this problem exists in the values of the services of 30 branches of the intellectual sphere.

To confirm the above we can name what has been absent in the theory of accounting:

- accountancy in the sphere of enlightenment
- accountancy in the sphere of education
- accountancy in the sphere of entertainment
- accountancy in the sphere of mass media

These spheres of economy should involve their own specific accounting, different from that used in material production.

The intellectual sphere should have its own specific accounting, which differs from the accounting used in material production.

## THE NATIONAL ACCOUNTING SYSTEM IN THE INTELLECTUAL SPHERE

To begin, we should first say a few words about changing the national accounting system. Accounting should reflect the movement of the resources in the intellectual sphere:

- the uniqueness of creating intellectual values and services
- the uniqueness of distributing intellectual values and services
- the uniqueness of exchange intellectual values and services
- the uniqueness of consumption intellectual values and services

In general, the movement of intellectual values and services, in economic space can be presented as follows:

| Production process | Distribution process | Exchange process | Consumption process |
|---|---|---|---|
| Economic estimates of intellectual values | Economic estimates of intellectual values | Economic estimates of intellectual values | Economic estimates of intellectual values |
| Economic estimates of intellectual services taking into account the spare time resource $A_{STP}$ | Economic estimates of intellectual services taking into account the spare time resource $A_{STP}$ | Economic estimates of intellectual services taking into account the spare time resource $A_{STP}$ | Economic estimates of intellectual services taking into account the spare time resource $A_{STP}$ |
| Economic estimates of intellectual product taking into account the spare time resource $A_{STP}$ | Economic estimates of intellectual product taking into account the spare time resource $A_{STP}$ | Economic estimates of intellectual product taking into account the spare time resource $A_{STP}$ | Economic estimates of intellectual product taking into account the spare time resource $A_{STP}$ |

I suggest we divide the intellectual sphere in three functional, different parts: education, enlightenment, entertainment.

The complex account of the movement of educational values and services can be presented as follows:

## THE VARIANT OF ESTIMATES OF EDUCATIONAL VALUES AND SERVICES IN THE ECONOMIC SPACE

| Production process | Distribution process | Exchange process | Consumption process |
|---|---|---|---|
| Economic estimates of educational values | Economic estimates of educational values | Economic estimates of educational values | Economic estimates of educational values |
| Economic estimates of educational services taking into account the spare time resource $A_{STP}$ | Economic estimates of educational services taking into account the spare time resource $A_{STP}$ | Economic estimates of educational services taking into account the spare time resource $A_{STP}$ | Economic estimates of educational services taking into account the spare time resource $A_{STP}$ |
| Economic estimates of the educational product taking into account the spare time resource $A_{STP}$ | Economic estimates of the educational product taking into account the spare time resource $A_{STP}$ | Economic estimates of the educational product taking into account the spare time resource $A_{STP}$ | Economic estimates of the educational product taking into account the spare time resource $A_{STP}$ |

### THE VARIANT OF ESTIMATES OF ENLIGHTENMENT VALUES AND SERVICES IN THE ECONOMIC SPACE

| Production process | Distribution process | Exchange process | Consumption process |
|---|---|---|---|
| Economic estimates of enlightenment values | Economic estimates of enlightenment values | Economic estimates of enlightenment values | Economic estimates of enlightenment values |
| Economic estimates of enlightenment services taking into account the spare time resource $A_{STP}$ | Economic estimates of enlightenment services taking into account the spare time resource $A_{STP}$ | Economic estimates of enlightenment services taking into account the spare time resource $A_{STP}$ | Economic estimates of enlightenment services taking into account the spare time resource $A_{STP}$ |
| Economic estimates of enlightenment product taking into account the spare time resource $A_{STP}$ | Economic estimates of enlightenment product taking into account the spare time resource $A_{STP}$ | Economic estimates of enlightenment product taking into account the spare time resource $A_{STP}$ | Economic estimates of enlightenment product taking into account the spare time resource $A_{STP}$ |

## THE VARIANT OF ESTIMATES OF ENTERTAINMENT VALUES AND SERVICES IN THE ECONOMIC SPACE

| Production process | Distribution process | Exchange process | Consumption process |
| --- | --- | --- | --- |
| Economic estimates of entertainment values | Economic estimates of entertainment values | Economic estimates of entertainment values | Economic estimates of entertainment values |
| Economic estimates of entertainment services taking into account the spare time resource $A_{STP}$ | Economic estimates of entertainment services taking into account the spare time resource $A_{STP}$ | Economic estimates of entertainment services taking into account the spare time resource $A_{STP}$ | Economic estimates of entertainment services taking into account the spare time resource $A_{STP}$ |
| Economic estimates of entertainment product taking into account the spare time resource $A_{STP}$ | Economic estimates of entertainment product taking into account the spare time resource $A_{STP}$ | Economic estimates of entertainment product taking into account the spare time resource $A_{STP}$ | Economic estimates of entertainment product taking into account the spare time resource $A_{STP}$ |

## THE VARIANT OF ESTIMATES OF INFORMATIONAL VALUES AND SERVICES IN THE ECONOMIC SPACE

| Production process | Distribution process | Exchange process | Consumption process |
|---|---|---|---|
| Economic estimates of informational values | Economic estimates of informational values | Economic estimates of informational values | Economic estimates of informational values |
| Economic estimates of informational services taking into account the spare time resource $A_{STP}$ | Economic estimates of informational services taking into account the spare time resource $A_{STP}$ | Economic estimates of informational services taking into account the spare time resource $A_{STP}$ | Economic estimates of informational services taking into account the spare time resource $A_{STP}$ |
| Economic estimates of informational product taking into account the spare time resource $A_{STP}$ | Economic estimates of informational product taking into account the spare time resource $A_{STP}$ | Economic estimates of informational product taking into account the spare time resource $A_{STP}$ | Economic estimates of informational product taking into account the spare time resource $A_{STP}$ |

Every position in this table needs to be created.

I suggest we name my system of national accounts non-traditional, it is, in fact, the truth.

Firstly, I suggest we get out of the frames of the formula: "The expenses-export".

Secondly, in the system of national accounts we will take in account the spare time of the population made up of intellectual services.

In the new system of national accounts, I suggest we use complex numbers. With their help, we can present the duality which exists in the economic process.

Thesis        The movement of intellectual values
Antithesis    The movement of intellectual services
Synthesis     The movement of the complex intellectual product

Before creating intellectual values and services using various resources

Thesis        Past labor
Antithesis    Present labor
Synthesis     Aggregate labor

The first and second logical structure, aforementioned, coincide with the logical structure of complex numbers.

Thesis        Real numbers—a
Antithesis    Imaginary numbers—bi
Synthesis     Complex numbers $Z = a + bi$

The coincidence of the first, second and third gives us the possibility to solve many problems in the accounting of the movement of resources.

# CHAPTER 1

## DUAL CHARACTER OF LABOR WHILE CREATING THE INTELLECTUAL PRODUCT

### A. PRODUCTION OF INTELLECTUAL VALUE

A social process of production of intellectual values (books, pictures, films, etc.) at a solitary level of consideration constitutes a system interaction of a solitary labor resource, a solitary system of labor means and instruments with a solitary subject of labor at a time unit. This interaction is schemed as follows:[1]

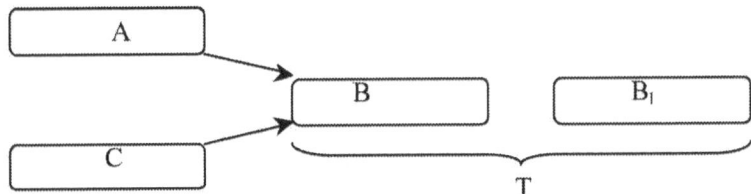

where

A—instruments of labor

B—subject of labor

C—labor resources

---

1   A book or a picture as such is a solitary product of labor created by a special type of an intellectual activity. Creation of intellectual values is maintained based on definite natural-logic Laws that are specific depending upon a intellectual activity type. There are ones for music and others for painting.

In the vector view, the process can be written down as in the following way:

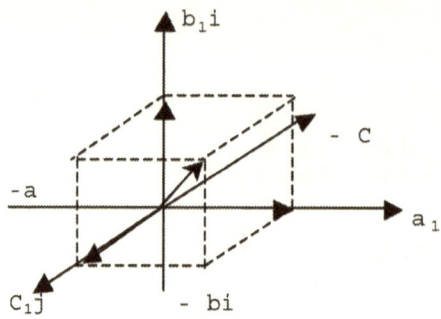

where

> A—instruments of labor connected with created intellectual value
> B—subject of labor connected with created intellectual values
> C—labor resources connected with created intellectual values
> T—time

$$Z = a + bi + Cj$$

The concrete labor of a composer or a writer attaches special specific properties to intellectual values, which distinguish these values from the others. Use value of the intellectual values is implemented provided the consumers of the goods purchase them. Otherwise, the values do not appear in this character quality.

## B.   PRODUCTION OF INTELLECTUAL SERVICE ELIGHTENMENT, EDUCATIONAL AND ENTERTAINMENT CHARACTER

A group of the intellectual sphere branches creates intellectual services in order to assimilate the population spare time resource. I propose these branches to be divided according to their functional indication:

Division II—increasing people's educational level

- «Education»
  - schools
  - colleges
  - universities

- «Enlightenment»;
  - «Culture»—a network of museums, libraries and club institutions,
  - «Art»—a network of theatres, circles, concert halls,
  - «Church»:—Orthodox, Catholic, Protestant, Muslim, etc.

Division III—creating services of an entertaining character
  - «Sport-entertaining» branch;
  - «Film Distribution»—a network of cinema halls;
  - «Radio Broadcasting»;
  - «TV Broadcasting».

The production process of intellectual services begins:

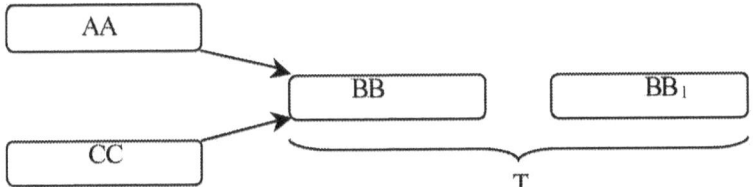

where
  AA—instruments of labor
  BB—subject of labor
  CC—labor resources

In the vector view, the process can be written down as in the following way:

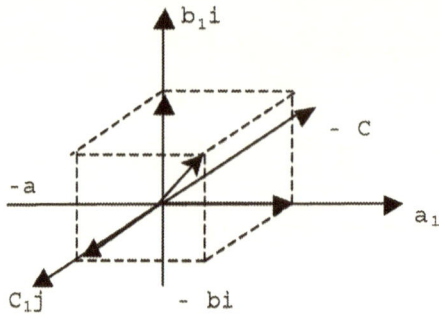

where

aa—instruments of labor connected with production of intellectual services

bb—subject of labor connected with production of intellectual services (assimilate the population spare time resource)

cc—labor resources connected with production of intellectual services

-    an owner sub-employs teachers, professors, etc., if an educational process is to be performed.[2]

T—time

In the vector view, the process can be written down as in the following way:

$$Z = aa + bbi + CCj$$

The concrete labor of the teachers, who create intellectual services with some different features in physics, chemistry and mathematics are three different types of intellectual services that possess specific use characteristics. Their consumption increases population knowledge and qualification. The services of a singer, a musician and an actor are three different types of intellectual services, that possess specific use (entertaining) characteristics.

An intellectual service comes out as a commodity provided it is a product of labor for the others, i.e. it has got a social use value. It is one thing to play Beethoven's sonata for yourself, and another thing the sonata to be reproduced for an audience in a hall. In the first case a proposed «service» does not come out as a social use value, in the second case it becomes such.

---

2    and football players, tennis players, singers, dancers and artists are to produce «Entertainment» services.

As a result of directed interaction of the factors (productive forces of the intellectual production) a specific service is created as per specific technology. The intellectual services are produced and created with a concrete labor during a specific time period, and they come out taking a specific non-material form —service form.

Should an intellectual service production have some commercial basis, a product of labor (an intellectual service) is sold out as a commodity and it is turned into money—M. And if the production is not a commercial one, intellectual services come out <u>as complimentary products—S.</u>

The quality of the services under consideration depends upon:

*first*, condition of the elements participating in a process,

*second*, character of the economic relations (progressive or regressive ones).[3]

## C.  PRODUCTION OF AN AGGREGATE INTELLECTUAL PRODUCT ELIGHTENMENT, EDUCATIONAL AND ENTERTAINMENT CHARACTER

The whole aggregate of the existing intellectual products created by the intellectual sphere is divided into two groups:

<u>I group</u>—intellectual values coming out as a thing, a subject (<u>intellectual values</u>). They are books, pictures, films, sculptures, TV sets, Radios, etc.

<u>II group</u>—intellectual services: lecturing, a film demonstration at a cinema hall, a church service, etc.

Intellectual values and services are organically connected.

---

3    It should be specially noted that without production of the intellectual services there is no consumption phase. An absence of a consumption phase of intellectual services conditions an absence of their production process. For instance, reading a lecture with no audience is a service in its potential and not an actual one.

In general, use value of an aggregate intellectual product is written down as a structure below:

## DIALECTICAL STRUCTURE OF THE «USE VALUE» CATEGORY OF THE INTELLECTUAL PRODUCT ELIGHTENMENT, EDUCATIONAL AND ENTERTAINMENT CHARACTER

**Thesis**      Use value of the intellectual values appears as a result of an inter-action (a motion) of the specific factors:

- means of labor connected with created intellectual values;

- instruments of labor connected with created intellectual values;

- subject of labor connected with created intellectual values;

- labor resource connected with created intellectual values.

**Antithesis**   Use value of an intellectual service (as a result of functioning of a concrete labor of a dancer, a singer, a musician, an actor) appears as a result of an inter-action of the specific factors:

- means of labor connected with created intellectual services;

- instruments of labor connected with created intellectual services;

- subject of labor connected with created intellectual services;

- labor resource connected with created intellectual services.

- employees of the intellectual sphere (a teacher, a dancer, a singer, a musician, etc.).

**Synthesis**   An aggregate use value of the intellectual product.

- means of labor connected with created aggregate intellectual product;

- instruments of labor connected with created aggregate intellectual product;

- subject of labor connected with created aggregate intellectual product;

- labor resource connected with created aggregate intellectual product.

A following dialectical scheme could be drawn up basing on the above:

---

### DIALECTICAL SCHEME
### OF A SOLITARY INTELLECTUAL PRODUCT ELIGHTENMENT,
### EDUCATIONAL AND ENTERTAINMENT CHARACTER

**Thesis:**      Solitary intellectual value.

**Antithesis:**  Solitary intellectual service.

**Synthesis:**   Solitary (aggregate) intellectual product (value and service).

---

A solitary-aggregate process of intellectual production should be understood as a directed purposeful process of an in-space-and-time interaction of the labor means and instruments of the solitary-aggregate system (SA-SML-IP), of a solitary-aggregate system of subjects of labor $(b + bb)i$ with a solitary-aggregate employee $(C + CC)j$ of an intellectual production per unit of time.

A distinction between production processes of intellectual values and services is based upon a distinction of the factors that form the productive forces of this type of production:

- means and instruments of labor of intellectual production Division 1 are different from the means and instruments of labor of intellectual production Division 2 & 3;

- subjects of labor of IP Division 1 are different from the subjects of labor of IP Division 2 & 3;

- labor resources of IP Division 1 are different from the labor resources of IP Division 2 & 3;

- production time of IP Division 1 is different from the production time in IP Division 2 & 3.

---

## DIALECTICAL STRUCTURE
## OF A SOLITARY INSTRUMENTS
## IN INTELLECTUAL PRODUCTION ELIGHTENMENT,
## EDUCATIONAL AND ENTERTAINMENT CHARACTER

**Thesis**      Solitary-aggregate system of labor means and instruments of intellectual value production (**a**).

**Antithesis**  Solitary-aggregate system of labor means and instruments of non-material intellectual service production (**aa**).

**Synthesis**   Solitary-aggregate system of labor means and instruments of intellectual production aaa = (a + aa)

---

---

## DIALECTICAL STRUCTURE
## OF A SOLITARY SYSTEM OF SUBJECTS OF LABOR
## OF INTELLECTUAL PRODUCTION ELIGHTENMENT,
## EDUCATIONAL AND ENTERTAINMENT CHARACTER

**Thesis**      Solitary-aggregate system of subjects of labor of intellectual value production (**bi**).

**Antithesis**  Solitary-aggregate system of subjects of labor of non-material intellectual service production (**bbj**).

**Synthesis**   Solitary-aggregate system of subjects of labor of intellectual production bbb = (bi + bbi)

where i—an imaginary unit

---

---

### DIALECTICAL STRUCTURE OF A SOLITARY WORKER OF INTELLECTUAL PRODUCTION ELIGHTENMENT, EDUCATIONAL AND ENTERTAINMENT CHARACTER

**Thesis**     Solitary-aggregate worker of an intellectual value (**C**).

**Antithesis**  Solitary-aggregate worker of an intellectual service (**CC**)

**Synthesis**   Solitary-aggregate worker of an intellectual production (CCC = Cj + CCj).

where i—an imaginary unit

---

---

### DIALECTICAL STRUCTURE OF THE «TIME» CATEGORY WITHIN INTELLECTUAL PRODUCTION ELIGHTENMENT, EDUCATIONAL AND ENTERTAINMENT CHARACTER

**Thesis**     Time of interaction of an intellectual value.

**Antithesis**  Time of interaction of an intellectual service.

**Synthesis**   Aggregate time of interaction of an intellectual product (value and service).

---

---

## DIALECTICAL STRUCTURE
## PROCESS OF LABOR CONNECTED WITH CREATED
## AGGREGATE INTELLECTUAL PRODUCT ELIGHTENMENT,
## EDUCATIONAL AND ENTERTAINMENT CHARACTER

**Thesis**     Socially productive intellectual process of labor connected with created intellectual values.

**Antithesis** Socially productive intellectual process of labor connected with created intellectual services.

**Synthesis**  Aggregate process of labor connected with created intellectual values.

---

---

## DIALECTICAL SCHEME ECONOMIC ESTIMATION
## PROCESS OF INTELLECTUAL PRODUCTION (IP)
## ELIGHTENMENT, EDUCATIONAL AND ENTERTAINMENT
## CHARACTER

**A. Thesis**       Economic estimation process of creation of the intellectual value.

$$Z = a + bi + Cj$$

**B. Antithesis**   Economic estimation process of creation of the intellectual service.

$$ZZ = aa + bbi + CCj$$

**C. Synthesis**    Aggregate economic estimation process of intellectual production as a whole.

$$ZZZ = aaa + bbbi + CCCj$$

Imaginary units—i, j—reveal different (heterogeneous) resources

---

# CHAPTER 2

# SOCIAL EVALUATION OF NTELLECTUAL SERVICES

**A. ANALYSIS OF THE INDICES USED IN THE INTELLECTUAL SPHERE**

**B. ASSIMILATED RESOURCE OF THE SPARE TIME OF THE POPULATION AS A SOCIAL INDICATOR**

**C. ASSIMILATION OF THE POPULATION'S SPARE TIME RESOURCE BY THE «ENLIGHTENMENT, EDUCATIONAL AND ENTERTAINMENTBRANCHES»**

## A. ANALYSIS OF INDICES USED IN THE INTELLECTUAL SPHERE

An analysis of economic literature shows, economists have only now come to a single opinion about what makes a purposeful guideline for «Education», «Enlightenment», «Culture», «Art», «Sports enlightenment and entertainment», «Church», «Film Distribution», «TV Broadcasting» and «Radio Broadcasting» branches. These branches now utilize indices such as «man-visit», «man-service», «man-place», «man-lecture», «man-enlightenment and entertainment», «TV-viewer», «Radio-listener» as units to measure the results of their activity. Inadequate existing indices means that labor in the intellectual sphere is indirectly reflected in aggregate indices in the statistics. For instance, a «man-visit» can be both 30-minutes one and 90-minutes long, yet the statistics treat these two different values as identical. Such inaccuracies in intellectual sphere enterprises have adverse economic and social consequences.

Use of the «man-visit» index is criticized by many researchers of social problems. For instance, Professor G.T. Shooter believes that «man-service» as a yardstick to measure the success of culture enterprises «does not reflect clearly enough the real state of affairs, nor does it account for the territorial, regional and other distinctions between different people and their living conditions».[4]

Professor B. A. Smith thinks that an unequal reflection of the social target causes purposeless planning: «it is becoming rather common to transfer from a purposeless method of programming and planning to the utilization of different program ideas earmarked in the sphere of culture».[5]

It is pointless to utilize a «man-visit» index as a purposeful guideline, given that it does not reflect the absolute volume of the social effect created by intellectual sphere enterprises and institutions. Hence, instead of the above index, I propose **an assimilated resource of the «spare time of the population» (STP)** to be utilized as a social index in the development of «Education», «Enlightenment», «Culture», «Art», «Sport entertainment», «Church», «Film Distribution», «TV Broadcasting» and «Radio Broadcasting».

The apparent simplicity of the concept hides many problems not solved within the framework of a new economic theory applied to the intellectual sphere of social production.

## A.  SPARE TIME OF THE POPULATION AS AN ECONOMIC RESOURCE

Some years ago I studied the work of two American professors Campbell R. McConnell & Stanley L. Brue «Economics, Principles, Problems, and Policies.» I was interested in how they solved the problem presented by spare time in American economic theory. They declared that the «increased volume of spare time, naturally, has had a very positive effect on our well-being. However, the system of social accounting in the USA doesn't reflect complete well being, for it doesn't consider the circumstances».[6]

Yet this is the most valuable resource of any society, since spare time constitutes what we can spend at will for our own purposes. The spare time of one individual amounts to 125,000–130,000 hours over a period of 60 years.

Initial calculations establish that the US adult population disposes of 900 billion hours of leisure time. If you include children, this amounts to an estimated

---

4    Shooter G.T. A Social Infra Structure: Essence and ways of development. M., p. 105.

5    Social Research, M., №_3, p.83.

6    «Economics: Principles, Problems, and Policies» Campbell R. McConnell, Stanley L. Brue (p. 142)

1500 billion hours per annum. In periods of mass unemployment, these numbers are considerably greater.

But the spare time of the population is an economic resource of considerable social value. Really the spare time of the population should be calculated as part of the Gross Domestic Product (GDP). However, so far it has been excluded from consideration of the activities of the people of a region or a town. Ignoring the intellectual services when estimating the Gross Domestic Product creates many problems for the whole business of providing socio-economic targets for development. For instance, it is not clear what proportion of the population's spare time constitutes a social asset and what proportion does not.

What direction should we take to promote the proportion of spare time as contributing to social wealth? We will not make notable improvements in planning, organising and administering the intellectual sphere branches until adequate replies are provided for the questions raised above.

Worst of all they divert attention from the need to estimate the actual economics involved in them. «A man-visit» index and other indices of this kind cannot serve as an economic guideline for the development of the activities under consideration.

## B.   ASSIMILATED RESOURSE OF THE SPARE TIME OF THE POPULATION AS A SOCIAL INDICATOR

The assimilated resource of the population's spare time, hourly, daily and annually are the targets for services of the intellectual sphere. Using an indicator of time to estimate the activities of the said branch enterprises, supersedes the varying quality of the services and their specific character, leading to a unique and single measurability. I am sure that my opponents will think that my suggestion of using a time parameter to determine an absolute volume of intellectual production services has its shortcomings. If a film or show is of poor quality or bad, a number of dissatisfied viewers may leave early i.e. they interrupt the process of intellectual servicing. Hence, there would be a divergence between the statistics and the reality. [7]

For instance, a portion of vegetables may be of bad quality and unserviceable to the population. In other words, there is also some divergence between the

---

7    Indeed, it may occur, but one should not forget that the statistics account for the per capita consumption of material values (vegetables, fruits, etc.) with the same approximate expenses.

statistics and the actual data of material production. Inserting the assimilated STP resource (or absolute volume of intellectual services) as one component of an aggregate result of activities in a region, or town, corresponds completely to elementary economic logic.

## C.  ASSIMILATION OF PEOPLE'S SPARE TIME RESOURCE BY SECONDARY SCHOOLS IN THE USA

There are 105,500 schools in the US education system, with 44 million pupils in 1986—27.2 million in primary classes and 16.8 million in secondary schools.[8]

On the basis that the assimilated spare time resource by primary schools comes to 700 hours per annum and 1200 hours, by secondary schools, an assimilated resource of US children's spare time by secondary schools comes to:

| | |
|---|---|
| 27.2 million men x 700 hours | = 19 billion men-hours, |
| 16.8 million men x 1200 hours | = 20 billion men-hours |
| **Total:** | 39 billion men-hours |

## ASSIMILATION OF THE PEOPLE'S SPARE TIME RESOURCE BY HIGHER EDUCATION SERVICES IN THE USA

There are about 3,300 different type institutes with over 12 million students in the USA. Three per cent of GDP is spent on higher schooling.

The cost for one student's education comes to US$ 12-15,000 per annum or US$ 20,000 at more «prestigious» institutions.

According to preliminary calculations, 9.2 billion hours of people's spare time are assimilated by university and college services in the USA.

---

8    The state expenses for the branch came to USD 145.5 billion, 93 per cent met by the state and local authorities, while the government met only 6.2 per cent of the expenses.

## D. THE EXPENSES IN THE INTELLECTUAL SPHERE

Today the intellectual sphere expenses were believed to be the expenses of the servicing branches only:

Should we proceed the intellectual sphere to consist of the branches producing values and services, the expenses of the sphere under consideration are to be calculated as follows:

*Scheme №*

### DIALECTICAL STRUCTURE
### OF LABOR EXPENSES WHILE PRODUCING «AN AGGREGATE INTELLECTUAL PRODUCT» ELIGHTENMENT, EDUCATIONAL AND ENTERTAINMENT CHARACTER

THESIS

### DIALECTICAL STRUCTURE
### OF LABOR EXPENSES WHILE CREATING INTELLECTUAL VALUES

**Thesis**  Expenses of past labor while creating intellectual values

**Antithesis**  Expenses of direct labor while creating intellectual values

**Synthesis**  Expenses of aggregate labor (past and direct) while creating intellectual values

ANTITHESIS

### DIALECTICAL STRUCTURE
### OF LABOR EXPENSES WHILE CREATING INTELLECTUAL SERVICES

**Thesis**  Expenses of past labor while creating the intellectual services

**Antithesis**  Expenses of direct labor while creating the intellectual services

**Synthesis**  Expenses of aggregate labor (past and direct) while creating the intellectual services

SYNTHESIS

## DIALECTICAL STRUCTURE
## OF THE EXPENSES WHILE A PRODUCTION OF «AN AGGREGATE INTELLECTUAL PRODUCT»

**Thesis**      Aggregate expenses of the past labor while creating «an aggregate intellectual product»

**Antithesis**   Aggregate expenses of the direct labor while creating «an aggregate intellectual product»

**Synthesis**   Aggregate expenses of the labor (past and direct) while creating «an aggregate intellectual product»[9]

*Scheme №*

## DUAL STRUCTURE
## OF THE INTELLECTUAL SPHERE EXPENSES ELIGHTENMENT, EDUCATIONAL AND ENTERTAINMENT CHARACTER

1.  Expenses of the first group of intellectual sphere branches which create material intellectual values:

    • expenses for a book production,

    • expenses for a magazine production,

    • expenses for a film production,

    • expenses for Radio broadcasting,

    • expenses for TV broadcasting

*Z Expenses of the branches producing intellectual values*

---

9    In reality the expenses of the intellectual sphere are not limited to the expenses of the above branches. Its expenses constitute a part of the common expenses of society and the intellectual services created in the «Church» frames are a part of the general result of the intellectual sphere.

Apart from the above, the common expenses of the intellectual production do not account for the expenses of the branches that produce intellectual values like newspapers, magazines, books, films, TV sets, Radios, etc. In other words, if we do not account the expenses of the branches producing the intellectual values in the general structure of the intellectual sphere expenses, it would be a considerable logical mistake that would lead to inadequate financing of the intellectual sphere and of an economy as a whole.

2.  Expenses of the second group of the intellectual sphere branches which create material intellectual values:

- expenses for «Education»
- expenses for «Enlightenment»
- expenses for «Culture», «Art»,
- expenses for «Sport-entertaining branch»,
- expenses for «Church»,
- expenses for «Film distribution»,
- expenses for «TV broadcasting»,
- expenses for «Radio broadcasting»,

***ZZ Expenses of the branches producing intellectual services***

3.  <u>otal: Expenses of the intellectual sphere</u> **ZZZ** = $Z$ + $Zi$ (Expenses of the branches producing the intellectual values plus expenses of the branches producing the intellectual services)

## C. DUAL CHARACTER OF THE «EXCHANGE» RELATION IN THE INTELLECTUAL SPHERE OF PRODUCTION

It is necessary to consider a single aspect of the «exchange» relation and to consider both horizontal and vertical structures to answer the questions above.

### 1) HORIZONTAL STRUCTURE OF THE «EXCHANGE» RELATIONS

The «exchange» relations are possible to be written down as follows at their elementary level of understanding:

**Var. 1 Material values A**    → *are exchanged to* →  **Material values B**
**Var. 2 Material values B**    → *are exchanged to* →  **Services A**
**Var. 3 Services A**           → *are exchanged to* →  **Services B**

In an every day practice the material values are exchanged for the intellectual services as against the scheme below:

**Material values→** *are exchanged to* →          **Intellectual services**
**(cost evaluat\on)**                              **(men-visits)**

The above scheme includes cost evaluation of the material values, but cost evaluation of the intellectual services is not available. An activity estimate of the branches producing the intellectual services has so far possessed a very high level of subjectively, which finally leads to an inadequate exchange. The above given scheme should be modified as follows:

**Material values**              →**Money** →          **Intellectual services**
**(cost evaluation)**                                **(cost evaluation)**

Thus, exchange relations are transferred from a subjective plane of consideration into an objective one.

The services of a singer and a baker are directed to meet different human needs. Bread cannot replace a romantic sound. But, as production costs are incurred in the first and second cases, bread and romance are homogeneous by their expense indication. Shortly, the material and intellectual values are heterogeneous, on one hand, and, on the other hand, they are homogeneous on basis of their expense indication. Thus, it is possible to exchange them in a definite proportion. An ability of one commodity and service to be exchanged in a definite proportion for another commodity and service determines the essence of the «exchange value» category.

If, for instance, 10 intellectual services should be conventionally exchanged for other commodities and services in a following proportion:

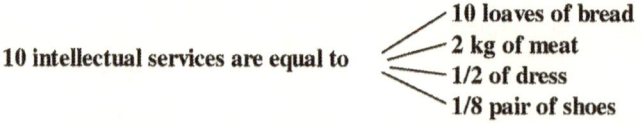

an exchange correlation reveals that an equal quantity of social labor is enclosed in an intellectual service accounting for a coefficient (10, 2, 1/2, 1/8).

The ratios change depending on the quality of an intellectual service and terms of a market. For example, a show of Moiseev's dance group is a service of one quality, and «Entertainment» services of a regional club dance group is a service of completely different quality. An exchange proportion in the first and second cases would be considerably different.

So then, an intellectual service is to be concrete (the one produced with a concrete labor), and, the expenses of its creation are to come out as expenses socially recognized. It is the only case an «exchange» phase can take place. The above is drawn down in a logical structure as follows:

*Table № 1*

## 1. Thesis

| Concrete labor | → Use value of intellectual values | |
|---|---|---|
| Expenses to produce the intellectual values | → Value of intellectual values | Exchange value of intellectual values |

## 2.Antithesis

| Concrete labor | → Use value of an intellectual service | |
|---|---|---|
| Expenses to produce the intellectual services | → Value of an intellectual service | Exchange value of intellectual services |

## 3.Synthesis

| Concrete labor | → Aggregate use value of an intellectual product | |
|---|---|---|
| Expenses to produce the aggregate intellectual product | → Aggregate value of an intellectual product | Exchange value of the aggregate intellectual product |

It is obvious on the basis of the above that «an exchange value» has a dual logical structure:

<u>Scheme № 12</u>

## DIALECTICAL STRUCTURE
## OF THE EXCHANGE VALUE OF AN INTELLECTUAL PRODUCT

**Thesis**       Exchange value of an intellectual value

**Antithesis**   Exchange value of an intellectual service

**Synthesis**    Aggregate exchange value of an intellectual product (intellectual value and intellectual service)

The above given structure reflects the essence of the «exchange value» category in the intellectual sphere in a condensed form. Should the category be considered extensively now:

<u>Scheme № 13</u>

## GENERAL SCHEME
## OF ECONOMIC PROPERTIES OF THE INTELLECTUAL VALUES

**Thesis**       Use value of the intellectual values

**Antithesis**   Value of the intellectual values

**Synthesis**    Exchange value of the intellectual values

## DUAL STRUCTURE
## OF ECONOMIC PROPERTIES OF INTELLECTUAL SERVICES

**Thesis**       Use value of an intellectual service

**Antithesis**   Value of an intellectual service

**Synthesis**    Exchange value of an intellectual service

# DUAL STRUCTURE
# OF ECONOMIC PROPERTIES OF THE INTELLECTUAL PRODUCT

**Thesis**     Aggregate use value of the intellectual product

**Antithesis**  Aggregate value of the intellectual product

**Synthesis**  Aggregate exchange value of the intellectual product

*Table № 2*

### DIALECTICAL SCHEME OF «EXCHANGE» RELATIONS
### OF THE INTELLECTUAL PRODUCTION

A) Exchange of intellectual values for other values and services

| Thesis | Past labor expenses while creating intellectual values | $\equiv$ * ratio A1 | Past labor expenses while creating values and services of other production spheres |
|---|---|---|---|
| **Antithesis** | Direct labor expenses while creating intellectual values | $\equiv$ ratio B1 | Direct labor expenses while creating values and services of other production spheres |
| **Synthesis** | Aggregate labor expenses while creating intellectual values | $\equiv$ ratio C1 | Aggregate labor expenses while creating values and services of other production spheres |

B) Exchange of intellectual services for other values and services

| **Thesis** | Past labor expenses while creating intellectual services | $\equiv$ ratio A2 | Past labor expenses while creating values and services of other production spheres |
|---|---|---|---|
| **Antithesis** | Direct labor expenses while creating intellectual services | $\equiv$ ratio B2 | Direct labor expenses while creating values and services of other production spheres |
| **Synthesis** | Aggregate labor expenses while creating intellectual services | $\equiv$ ratio C2 | Aggregate labor expenses while creating values and services of other production spheres |

C) Exchange of intellectual product for other values and services

| **Thesis** | Aggregate past labor expenses while creating intellectual product | ≡ ratio A3 | Past labor expenses while creating values and services of other production spheres |
|---|---|---|---|
| **Antithesis** | Aggregate direct labor expenses while creating intellectual product | ≡ ratio B3 | Direct labor expenses while creating values and services of other production spheres |
| **Synthesis** | Aggregate labor expenses while creating intellectual product | ≡ ratio C3 | Aggregate labor expenses while creating values and services of other production spheres |

## E. DUAL CHARACTER OF «DISTRIBUTION» RELATIONS IN INTELLECTUAL SPHERE OF PRODUCTION

The distribution relations constitute a specific type of the economic relations, and the essence is to distribute material, labor, financial and other resources. Any research of the distribution relations cannot be limited to the frames of material production only. The relations take place in every relatively autonomous sphere of social production: material, intellectual, public health, transport, military and administration.

An analysis of economic literature that «distribution» relations (a distribution mechanism) are not developed for the intellectual sphere of production and this leads to an indirect coordination of the activities of such branches as «Education», «Culture», «Art», «TV and Radio Broadcasting» and others.

The low quality of distribution relations in the intellectual sphere forces us to carry out their further elaboration and development. Moreover, we should bear in mind that distribution relations are not «one-sided». They possess both horizontal and vertical structure of their formation.

## 1) HORIZONTAL STRUCTURE OF DISTRIBUTION RELATIONS IN INTELLECTUAL SPHERE

The essence of the horizontal structure of the relations under consideration lies in distributing one-type resources in time and space.

The distribution relation in the branches producing the intellectual values are:
- distribution of resources in book publishing;
- distribution of resources in magazine editing;
- distribution of resources in film production;
- distribution of resources in the production of video and radio equipment.

The distribution relation in the branches producing the intellectual services are:
- distribution of «Education» resources;
- distribution of «Enlightenment» resources;
- distribution of «Culture» and «Art» resources;
- distribution of Sport-entertainment branch resources;
- distribution of Church resources;
- distribution of film distribution resources;
- distribution of «TV Broadcasting» resources;
- distribution of «Radio Broadcasting» resources.

## 2) VERTICAL STRUCTURE OF DISTRIBUTION RELATIONS IN INTELLECTUAL SPHERE

If we assort that the intellectual production consists of three relatively autonomous divisions of production, the distribution relations would have a vertical structure. The same can be written down as follows:

*Scheme № 14*

### DIALECTICAL STRUCTURE OF DISTRIBUTION RELATIONS IN INTELLECTUAL SPHERE

**Thesis:**     «Distribution» within intellectual production Division I.

a) «Distribution» of means and instruments of labor of intellectual production Division 1.

b) «Distribution» of labor resources functioning in intellectual production Division I.

c) «Distribution» of the subjects of labor of intellectual production Division I.

d) «Distribution» of labor results of intellectual production Division I in time and space.

**Antithesis:** A) «Distribution» within intellectual production Division II.

a) «Distribution» of means and instruments of labor of intellectual production Division II.

b) «Distribution» of labor resources functioning in intellectual production

c) «Distribution» of labor results of intellectual production Division II in time and space.


B) «Distribution» within intellectual production Division III.

a) «Distribution» of means and instruments of labor of intellectual production Division III.

b) «Distribution» of the labor resources functioning in intellectual production Division III.

c) «Distribution» of the labor results of intellectual production Division III in time and space.

**Synthesis:**    «Distribution» in intellectual production.

a) «Distribution» of means and instruments of labor of IP Divisions I, II & III.

b) «Distribution» of labor resources of IP Divisions I, II & III.

c) «Distribution» of subjects of labor of IP Divisions I, II & III.

d) «Distribution» of labor results of IP Divisions I, II & III.


## E. DUAL CHARACTER OF THE «CONSUMPTION» RELATION IN THE INTELLECTUAL SPHERE OF PRODUCTION

## 1) HORIZONTAL STRUCTURE OF «CONSUMPTION» RELATIONS IN THE INTELLECTUAL SPHERE

The essence of the horizontal structure of «consumption» relations in this specific sphere is that they are implemented in the «field» of one type of the intellectual values, of one type of the intellectual services in time and space, in the context of the branches forming the sphere.

### The branches producing intellectual values:

- book production;
- magazine, journal production;
- film production
- production of video and audio equipment.

### The branches producing intellectual services:

- «Enlightenment», «Education», «Culture», «Art» aiming to increase the professional skills of the population.

### The branches producing entertainment services:

- «Sports-entertaining branch»;
- «Film distribution»;
- «TV Broadcasting»;
- «Radio Broadcasting».

## 2) VERTICAL STRUCTURE OF THE «CONSUMPTION» RELATIONS IN THE INTELLECTUAL SPHERE

Should we assort that the intellectual production consists of the three relatively autonomous spheres of production, the «consumption» relations process is possible to be written down as follows:

*Scheme № 15*

### DUAL STRUCTURE
### OF THE «CONSUMPTION» RELATIONS
### IN THE INTELLECTUAL SPHERE

**Thesis**      «Consumption» in Division 1 of the intellectual production

**Antithesis**  a) «Consumption» in Division 2 of the intellectual production

b) «Consumption» in Division 3 of the intellectual production

**Synthesis**   Aggregate «consumption» in Divisions 1, 2 & 3 of the intellectual production

The structure has a detailed form:

*Scheme № 16*

## DUAL STRUCTURE
## OF CONSUMPTION IN THE INTELLECTUAL PRODUCTION (CIP)

**Thesis**     «Consumption» within Division 1 of the intellectual production.

a) «consumption» of the means and instruments of labor of intellectual production Division 1

b) «consumption» of the labor resources functioning in intellectual production Division 1

c) «consumption» of the items of labor of intellectual production Division 1

d) «consumption» of the labor results of intellectual production Division 1 in time and space Production

**Antithesis** **a)** «Consumption» within Division 2 of the intellectual production.

a) «consumption» of the means and instruments of labor of intellectual production Division 2

b) «consumption» of the labor resources functioning in intellectual production Division 2

c) «consumption» of the labor results of intellectual production Division 2 in time and space

**b)** «Consumption» within Division 3 of the intellectual production.

a) «consumption» of the means and instruments of labor of intellectual production Division 3

b) «consumption» of the labor resources functioning in intellectual production Division 3

c) «consumption» of the labor results of intellectual production Division 3 in time and space

**Synthesis**  «Consumption» in the intellectual production.

a) «consumption» of the means and instruments of labor of intellectual production Divisions 1, 2 & 3

b) «consumption» of the labor resources of intellectual production Divisions 1, 2 & 3

c) «consumption» of the items of labor of IP Divisions 1, 2 & 3

d) «consumption» of the labor results of IP Divisions 1, 2 & 3

The relations are rather specific: productive consumption (of the books, pictures, musical instruments, video and audio tapes, etc.) and personal (unproductive) consumption of the stated values. Besides, on one hand, consumption of intellectual services is maintained to increase professional skills (education) and, on the other hand, to entertain people.

The above has its own logical structure as follows:

*Scheme № 17*

### DIALECTICAL STRUCTURE OF «CONSUMPTION» IN THE INTELLECTUAL SPHERE AS PER FUNCTIONAL INDICATIONS

**Thesis**      Production consumption of intellectual values and services.

**Antithesis**  Non-production consumption of the intellectual values and services.

**Synthesis**   Aggregate consumption of the intellectual values and services (a production and non-production).

# CHAPTER 3

## ANALYSIS OF INDICES USED
## IN THE INTELLECTUAL SPHERE

**A. PROBLEMS OF AN ECONOMIC EVALUATION OF «EDUCATION» SERVICES**

**B. PROBLEMS OF AN ECONOMIC EVALUATION OF «ENLIGHTENMENT» SERVICES**

**C. NEW ECONOMIC STRUCTURE OF AN INTELLECTUAL SERVICE**

## A. PROBLEMS OF AN ECONOMIC EVALUATION OF «EDUCATION» SERVICES

Academician S.G. Strumilin has carried out considerable studies of the economic problems of education. He applies question of «requirement» to the repayment of expenses on education and the public education optimum for a society in a proper economic approach.

One of his main contributions to the research of public education problems, was that he was the first to consider the economic aspect of the branch and to set out the basic characteristics of its organization. In particular, he used annual duration of education, full labor expenses in the branch, wages and surplus product created by the educated and trained workers in the material sphere of social production broadly. He put the labor quality a first grade worker as «a tred» (a labor unit) to calculate wage rates for teachers. He estimated labor complexity a 3.3, 3.7 and 7.4 treds for first grade teachers, secondary education teacher's and university teachers, respectively.

Based on the huge number of statistics S.G. Strumilin came to the conclusion that «one year of school education gives a qualification approximately 2.6 times higher than that of manual labor practice … Hence, everything given to future worker in school between ages of 7-16 is their net profit in any future professional activity».[10] The research was carried out to determine the influence of educational qualifications on the workforce and its social significance.

He determined the expenses required for education and established the general increase in national income spent on this activity in the material sphere of production. S.G. Strumilin calculated that the means directed to develop popular education equaled 23 per cent of National Income. Professor V.A. Zhamin calculated, that it came to 27 per cent of the National Income. A further investigation of the effectiveness of popular education effectiveness reveals that its share of national income came to 38.2 per cent for the whole volume of the material sphere.

According to Professor V.A. Zhamin «expenses on education are a kind of capital investment, that is compensated for by an increase in production output, working time, and expansion in the different kinds and quality of production, at a time when production manufacture is in decline … A rising level of education results in an increase in the National Income, given that complicated labor creates more cost than simple labor because it utilizes greater knowledge, thanks to better employee education. The disparity between the income and expenditure on education makes up the most general indicator of effectiveness of education expenses».

The researchers of the economic problems in the «Education» branches face difficulty in the large number of indicators not connected to each other, which do not allow a qualitative socio-economic analysis of the branches' organization, necessary to set up an inter-branch economic balance with an account for the results of their activity.

Lack of any elaboration of the socio-economic evaluation of «Education» products of labor makes it impossible to maintain any planned development. A shortage in the criteria of economic effectiveness leads to serious omissions and a disproportionate list of experts with higher and special secondary education. *«One of the reasons of interfering in… preparing experts… is that the organizational structure of administration of high schools and universities is not perfect. This leads to regional and departmental tendencies in the preparation of experts. A rational scheme to allocate high schools and universities all over the country has not yet been developed. As a result one can see a parallelism in the prepara-*

---

10    Academician S.G.Strumilin's article «Economic value of popular education». P 9-10.

*tion of experts of the same grade and profession in several education institutions in a country and as the Departments have high schools and universities under them they do not have the will to develop optimum forms of concentration and specialization in training experts. They would rather prepare different professional staff in small quantities. Besides expert preparation of a large number of narrow professions, when a group of 25 students is admitted creates big difficulties in the distribution and utilization of the experts».*

Whilst analyzing indices of the activity results of the popular education system, Professor V.A. Zhamin notes that *«different indices are used in economic and financial plans, which do not sufficiently compliment each other, or to satisfy different types of institution. An economic development plan calculates variable and fixed indices of popular education. The latter are: working out new pupil places, the number of pupils in school operation at a year end; admittance and output of students in high schools, colleges and universities. Variable indices are number of classes at the beginning of an educational year in secondary schools and the annual number of students trained for new professions».*

V.A. Zhamin proposes « ... a group of pupils and students» be used as a unique and main index. «The index determines all others; a number of groups, teachers and service personnel, and volume of expenses all depend on the index». But there is no unique system of characteristics of the socio-economic effectiveness of educational institutions in the system of main indices, and it complicates a solution of the questions about their rational organisation.

Professor V. Komarov, whilst analyzing the problems of the branches «Education», found that expenses on education were increased by 3.4 times, and its proportion of national income, (formed by the material sphere of production at the expense of the growth of labor qualifications in it) increased by 4 times.[11] He proposed that effective capital investment in «Education» should be calculated by a system of formulas as follows:

$$E1 = \frac{\Delta V_{MS}}{\Delta C_{SE}} \quad , \quad E2 = \frac{\Delta NP_{MS}}{\Delta C_{SE}}$$

in which

---

11    Komarov V. Economic Effectiveness of education. «Questions on economics», p. 64, 65.

- volume of an increase in GDP, a net product in the material sphere of production;

- size of capital investment in a system of popular education.

Professor V. Komarov proposes to calculate the cost of popular education on the basis of the expenses connected to the usage of materials and technology and the wages (a required product) of the branch. In his preliminary calculations, the cost of education accumulated by the workers in the material sphere of production, (including professional ones), came to $ 260-266 billion.[12] The potential is to be treated rationally, as «treatment of any country's intellectual potential without proper economy … causes great economic and moral damages to society».[13]

Professor V. Komarov's position on the questions of determining a country's intellectual potential is limited to the material sphere of production. Yet the same potential lies in the intellectual, public health and military spheres, etc. A «narrow» focus on the problems of forming a country's intellectual makes it difficult to determine the full volume of these services, which would allow us to consider this labor on a par with the material and technical spheres of production and find out a portion of GDP (at its widest sence) being produced at expense of public education branches.

However, he does not account for:

1.  development of the following factors in current and long-term planning:

    - means and instruments of labor of education;

    - labor resources of education.

2.  the economic results of the « education» activities are indirectly determined in material production;

3.  a purposeful function of « education»;

4.  developed economic structure of the education services;

5.  spare time resource of the population assimilated by «education» is not included in the cost of the branch services;

6.  there is no elaboration of the criteria of the socio-economic effectiveness of direct labor, past labor, and aggregate labor in «education», or the effectiveness criteria of capital investments in their development;

---

12  See V. Komarov Economic Effectiveness of education. «Questions on economics», p. 8.

13  M.V Zimyanin. Economic Effectiveness of education. «Questions on economics», p. 33.

7.  sufficient economic and mathematical methods in administrating the branches of «education».

«Education» should aspire to the optimum condition and state, i.e. to keeping expenses of its outer function to a minimum. A co-measurement of the «result» and «expense» functions in the «education branches» is not carried out, because a «result» function is changed with an «expense» function. What do we mean by saying the outer function being changed for an inner one? We mean the fact that a volume of services is frequently substituted with a volume of expenses connected with «education branches». Such substitution creates the paradox that: the worse an institution works, the higher its volume of production expenses, and, consequently, the higher its volume of services granted to people and the higher our intellectual security is. In other words, the worse these institutions work, the better it is for us.

## B.  PROBLEMS OF AN ECONOMIC EVALUATION OF «ENLIGHTENMENT» SERVICES

I propose that the formula $C + V + M = P$ for the economic estimation of the branches of «enlightenment and education». Looks as follows:

$$C + V + M = \text{«visit»} \qquad\qquad 1.$$

in which

C—transferred past labor;

V—wages;

M—profit.

On the one hand, the formula uses economic categories, and on the other hand, it uses a theoretical unit of measurement. Should, for instance, two equations be executed in equation 1:

$$1)\ C + V = \text{«visit»} - M,$$
$$2)\ C + M = \text{«visit»} - V,$$

the first variant takes a surplus value (M) away from «visit», and the second variant takes wages (V) out of «visit».

The main limitation of «visit» is that it does not express the cost of the newly created service, thus it cannot serve as an indicator of labor input in enterprises intellectual services to Gross Domestic Product and National Income.

Net «visit» indicator has a negative impact on all sides of these enterprises' economic activities. For instance, due to the above, schemes of simple and an expanded reproduction of the intellectual sphere do not interact clearly with the resources of material production and vice versa.

These arguments prove that a «visit» index and similar ones cannot economically characterize labor results of the employees of enlightenment and education objectively. Moreover, they completely misrepresent an entire economic mechanism. And most depressingly of all is that they distract attention from estimating the actual economic tendencies taking place in them.

In conclusion, the «visit», «day», «lecture» indexes and analogous ones cannot estimate the economic development of these economic branches. Therefore, they are related to the «intermediate estimations» or «theoretical evaluations» of the activity results for the branches under consideration.

## NEW ECONOMIC STRUCTURE OF INTELLECTUAL SERVICE

While considering this huge theme, we must proceed on the basis that:

First:    economic theory of the intellectual sphere is to leave a zone of «exclusive logic» and the general principles of forming the expense and result portions of a product are to be used widely in it.

Second: The branches of «enlightenment and education» assimilate the spare time resource of the population. Thus, a formation logic for an economic structure of intellectual services is to be analogous with that existing for the mining industry. Mining material production, with the natural resources (oil, gas, coal, etc.) as the basic subject of their activities, include cost of the resource itself, together with C, V, to make the cost of the result of their activities. For this, we can modify a well-known formula as follows:

$$C + V + Pres = Pexp$$

in which

C—expenses of past labor connected to resource assimilation;

V—wages fund for workers assimilating the resource;

Pres—assimilated resource;

Pexp—cost of the product (an explored resource).

<u>Third</u>: <u>the spare time resource of population, assimilated by «enlightenment and education» is not included in the cost of intellectual services.</u>

<u>Fourth</u>: the assimilated resource of the population's spare time is to be estimated economically and included into the cost of a newly created product.

<u>Fifth</u>: the formula C + V + m = P misses <u>the main component—the assimilated resource of population spare time,</u> which all the factors of «enlightenment and education» are directed to assimilate—both past and direct labor.

<u>Sixth:</u> inclusion of this new compound (in the unit cost of measurement) would modify the structure of the proposed formula.

The formula would look as follows:

$$C + Vi + mk + A_{STP}j = P,$$

where

C—the past labor expenses;

Vi—wages;

mk —surplus product, profit of private schools, universities, etc.

$A_{STP}j$—the spare time resource of the population assimilated by enterprises producing intellectual services;

There are more than enough reasons to include the population spare time resource in the cost of intellectual services:

**first,** production of intellectual services is impossible without assimilating the population spare time resource, otherwise the service is not implemented;

**second,** consumption of intellectual services takes place during the process of creation;

**third,** the  beginning and end of intellectual service production coincide.

## SPARE TIME OF THE POPULATION AS AN ECONOMIC RESOURCE

Some years ago I studied the work of two American professors Campbell R. McConnell & Stanley L. Brue «Economics, Principles, Problems, and Policies.» I was interested in how they solved the problem presented by spare time in American economic theory. They declared that the «increased volume of spare time, naturally, has had a very positive effect on our well-being. However, the system of social accounting in the USA doesn't reflect complete well being, for it doesn't consider the circumstances».

## Assimilation of PEOPLE's spare time resource BY secondary schoolS IN the USA

There are 105,500 schools in the US education system, with 44 million pupils in 1986—27.2 million in primary classes and 16.8 million in secondary schools.

On the basis that the assimilated spare time resource by primary schools comes to 700 hours per annum and 1200 hours, by secondary schools, an assimilated resource of US children's spare time by secondary schools comes to:

| | |
|---|---|
| 27.2 million men x 700 hours | = 19 billion men-hours, |
| 16.8 million men x 1200 hours | = 20 billion men-hours |
| **Total:** | 39 billion men-hours |

## COST EVALUATION OF THE POPULATION SPARE TIME RESOURCE

A resource of spare time of population (STP) assimilated by the intellectual sphere branches is as much part of the wealth of a society as any other resource (oil, gas, coal mastered by the material production like any other branches). And as any wealth, STP has got its cost. What is the cost? It is not an easy task to determine a resource cost of STP. Leisure has an inner structure in terms of age, sex, education, etc.:

1) leisure time of children of pre-school and school age;

2) leisure time of students;

3) leisure time of the working part of population, etc.

Each of the above has to be separately evaluated and its own special ratios set up
whereby parameters of time may be converted into those of cost. The cost of
the resource naturally declines in times of mass unemployment and rises in
periods of maximum employment. When assessing an assimilated resource of
leisure, education must be considered as providing for the training of a person involved in producing socially valuable services. Another aspect of leisure
in the provision of «Sports-entertainment», «Culture», «Art», «Film distribution», «Church», «TV and Radio Broadcasting».

## COST EVALUATION OF THE INTELLECTUAL SERVICES IN THE USA

Leisure-time figures for the USA population are as follows:

| | |
|---|---|
| - pre-school institutions 20 bln. | man-hours; |
| - secondary schools | 39 bln hours; |
| - universities | 9.2 bln hours; |
| - TV and Radio Broadcasting | 170 bln hours; |

Total: 238.2 bln hours

Allowing for some 10-12 billion hours to be taken up by cinema and church
affairs per annum, the leisure time resource assimilated in the USA came to
250 billion hours in 1990. That year, the minimum salary was US $3.35 per
hour. The value of leisure time may therefore be evaluated as:

250 billion hours x US $3.35 = US $837.5 billion.

To the must be added the cost of labour and the wages of the employees producing intellectual services. In 1990 the expenses of education came to about US
$250 billion; the cost of «Culture», «Art», «Sports-entertainment», «Church»,
«Film Distribution», «TV Broadcasting» and «Radio Broadcasting» were
approximately US $150 billion.

Summing up the cost of the leisure resource of the USA population spare time
assimilated by the branches producing intellectual services, amounting to
expenses of US $400 billion. The total cost amounted to US $1237.5 billion
in 1990 and US $1462.5 billion in 1999, 15—20% of the GDP of the USA.
Thus, my conception makes it possible to measure the show services makes
it possible:

*First:* to calculate the intellectual proportion of the Gross Domestic Product (GDP);

*Second:* to eliminate a notable omission from calculations of GDP for the USA, and accordingly in many other countries.

## A. EDUCATIONAL SERVICES CREATED BY THE EXECUTIVE BRANCH OF POWER

In the present time, a significant part of the establishments of the educational branch are financed from the budget. The population consumes these services free-of-charge. The national deputies, say that the expenses allocated from the budget for the educated of the people, create a hole in the budget. How can we explain such certainty of the national deputies?

On the one hand, it is connected with the interdiction, which existed in the realization of the research of the government's economic problems. On the other hand, it can also be attributed to the narrow-mindedness of the economists, who have been brought up on the economic theories of the last centuries.

Still, the productive activity of the educational branches is not examined in the theory. For this reason, the education services are badly taken into account in the productive part of the executive branch of authority.

The executive branch of authority should be taken into account in the results of not only receipts from the taxes, but also of the educational services which it creates. In the new (extended) variant of the calculations of the result of the economical activities of executive branch of authority (taking into account educational services), every goes into its proper place.

## B. ENLIGHTENMENT SERVICES CREATED BY THE EXECUTIVE BRANCH OF POWER

Until recently, expenses, which are associated with the budget for enlightenment activity, were considered by many chiefs as «holes in the budget», which should be closed both on the right and left. Many academic economists recommend the reduction of expenses in the budget for enlightenment.

It is necessary to refuse such a traditional view, for the reason that the executive branch of authority does not take into account, in its results of economic activity, those services that create enlightenment. Today it is necessary to adjust the account of the services of enlightenment branches. Libraries, museums, the exhibition of representational and applied art, concert activity (national music, classical music, etc) are financed from the budget.

If the financing of the enlightenment branches occurs from the budget, the enlightenment services should be taken into account as a result of the activity of the executive branch of authority. Such consideration should be at the executive branch of authority.

This economic axiom of the executive branch of authority «number one».

## C. THE SERVICES OF THE FIRST NATIONAL TELEVISION CHANNEL

In many countries, the services of the first national television and the first radio channels are financed from the budget. In this variant, it is necessary to take into account the service of these channels, as a result of the activity of the executive authority. If the first channel is financed from the budget, all the services of this information channel should also be taken into account in the total amount of the services of the executive branch of authority. The television service should be estimated taking into account the mastered resource of the free time of these services $A_{STP}$.

# PART 2

## THE DOWJONES INDEX FOR MASS MEDIA SPHERE

Along with development of the state new branches of power: press industry, TV and Radio have been added to the three basic ones (a, b, C) according to journalists. Mass media is a new branch of power which has been shaped for the last 100 years.

It is difficult to give detailed account of the mass media influence the way it has been treated. It does not let itself be inscribed into traditional conceptions of state authority branches. Economic theory of mass media is not available.

Until recently we could only judge of the economic aspects of mass media by the rate of advertisement prices per minute, e.g. 50 or 100 thousand dollars. This knowledge however comprises only one hundredth of what is really going on in the economy of mass media.

Mass production of newspapers and magazines, radio and TV services makes it possible to single out production of information services as a separate block —information sphere of power.

By creating relevant services printed and mass media keeps people involved in the information process for two, three or five hours a day. It assimilates our spare time during which you become deprived of one or two degrees of freedom.

No one would deny the fact that mass media economy is existent. Moreover, it has its own structure, principles of organization, functioning peculiarities, rules which define the movement of streams of resources as well as specific financial models. I offer to apply production criteria in classifying new branches of power as regards the sphere of mass media.

Production of newspapers—fourth branch of power.

Production of Radio services—fifth branch of power.

Production of TV services—sixth branch of power.

Such a way of classification is not abstract and hence alienated from real life. We shall adhere to it and gradually specify one another aspect of the fourth, fifth and sixth branches of power.

First steps on the way of apprehending the economy of mass media should be taken towards researching the component parts of it.

General parameters of the fourth branch of power.

General parameters of the fifth branch of power.

General parameters of the sixth branch of power.

Newspapers

1,760 daily newspapers

61,5 million daily copies

70% of income comes from advertising, $ 11 billion annually;

30% of income comes from newspaper sales $ 4,7 billion annually

Magazines

2,394 publishers

37,000 titles, 50—with a circulation of over a million total income on advertising $ 2,1 billion

Radio Broadcasting

4497 stations;

2837 FM stations;

839 stations of social broadcasting;

4 commercial networks;

1 network of social broadcasting 425 million radio-receivers income from advertising is over $ 2,5 billion per annum

TV Broadcasting

728 commercial stations;

256 non commercial stations;

3 TV networks;

1 network of social (educational) broadcasting 121 million TV sets, covering 98% of the households total income from advertising is over $ 7,6 billion per annum

Cable TV

3,832 systems, including 8 largest companies cater for 37% of the subscribers
12 million subscribers

TV is the largest segment of the intellectual sphere judging by the extent of the people's involvement in the services rendered by it. In European countries at weekends alone, TV screens attract up to 200 million people. If we complement this figure with some 150 million more people enjoying TV services on weekdays, the amount of the human resource involved can hardly be compared with any other stream of human activity. Moreover, the given figures are significantly underestimated since they do not comprise the whole Europe with East-European countries.

At present in calculations related to the TV service market, it is customary to use such an indicator as the «number of TV viewers». However, it reveals only the statistical aspect of the stream of human resource serviced by the TV and is actually contracted due to the lack of the main component – the time factor.

Proceeding from the above, I suggest the following two indicators be considered:

Indicator 1. The number of TV viewers.

Indicator 2. The number of TV viewers adjusted for the time factor.

The completeness of the second indicator as compared with the first one lies in the fact that the statistical indicator is supplemented by the time factor which transfers TV viewers on to the plane of economic estimates.

Assuming that on Saturdays and Sundays about 200 million people spend 4 hours on an average watching TV, with Indicator 2 it comes to 800 million man-hours per day. Multiplying this quantity by 52 weeks a year we receive:

800 million man-hours X 52 Saturdays = 41,600,000,000 man-hours
800 million man-hours X 52 Sandays  = 41,600,000,000 man-hours

Hence preliminary calculations reveal that on Saturdays and Sundays alone 83.2 billion man-hours are assimilated annually.

By adding the amount of spare time of the population assimilated by the TV service Monday through Friday we shall have:

150 million people X 5 days X 4 hours X 52 = 156 billion man-hours per year.

Thus, assimilation of TV services in Europe comes to:

156 billion man-hours + 83.2 billion man-hours = 239.2 billion man-hours per annum.

Being precursory, these calculations, however, can tell a lot. They obviously have to be specified taking into account the expenses connected to the assimilation of the people's spare time resource. The latter can be regarded as unconventional, but it is exactly the same human resource.

In this case it acts as a «subject of labor» and is treated as an economic resource processed by specific intellectual means of influence. On these grounds, it should be included in the cost of TV services.

And there is nothing that would contradict the elementary economic logic: TV viewers act as one of the resources absorbed by the sphere of a specific service. The resource which should cost something. It cannot be worthless.

Now, if we use a conditional unit of currency in estimating 239.2 billion man-hours, it would be worth 239.2 billion. In these estimation, we shall have to deal either with a dollar, or a euro, of course.

Thus, having estimated one hour of spare time at one euro or one USD, the resource under consideration will be worth 239.2 billion euro or USD. And relevantly:

- 3 euro/hour will make up 717 billion euro;

- 5 euro/hour will come to 1 trillion 200 billion euro per annum.

To which of the following indicators in the European countries – GDP, NDP or NI—shall we add these values?
Which concrete indicator does this trillion refer to?

If to the GDP, then we shall also have to add to the above trillion expenses of the past (C) and direct (V) labor of the TV personnel.

If to the NDP, we shall add only the salaries of the TV personnel.

In relation to NI, we do not have to add any expenses of the TV stations to that same trillion. Consequently, it is necessary to specify how the human resource in question is being assimilated. 75% of spare time European TV viewers spend on watching American programs, i.e. the bulk of the people's spare time in Europe, is assimilated by the overseas TV technologies. Proceeding from this, 1 trillion 200 billion euro should be distributed:

- 75%, or 900 billion euro added to the US GNP;

- and only 25%, or 300 billion euro added to the US GDP of the West-European countries.

# CHAPTER 1

# THE FOURTH BRANCH OF POWER—PRESS INDUSTRY

## 1. PRESS INDUSTRY AS AN ECONOMIC SYSTEM

While examining economic problems of fourth branch of power it is necessary to point out that for the last 20 years the usage of computer engineering has brought about significant shrinkage of expenses in newspaper industry. We remember well the «Murdock effect» which changed traditional technologies of making up newspapers that resulted in reducing publishing expenditures.

Application of Internet services was another considerable event since if facilitated further reduction of expenses of newspaper production, distribution, exchange and consumption.

However, we shall not dwell on this question at length but concentrate upon those problems of economic theory of the fourth branch of power which have not been elaborated yet.

**www.NewspaperMagazineStockExchangeIndex.com**

The concentration and monopolisation of the printing industry is characteristic of a tendency to absorb separate publications and big publishing companies into huge monopolies. There are no enterprises among the leading monopolies that would limit themselves to just one type of production, newspapers in particular. As a rule, the monopolies are diversified, i.e. they are engaged with publishing various products: newspapers, magazines, books, they own radio- and TV-stations, cable TV systems, etc. They also own capital investments in different industries. The main monopolies of the natural press are massive conglomerates in the communication sector and they own practically all the leading bodies of the American Press.

The largest information propaganda monopolies in the USA are as follows. "Gannett Company" leads 90 newspapers with a circulation of over 5.7 million companies, out of the total number of dailies in America. A majority of them published in 33 states, have a comparatively small circulation. Cannett has published the massive national newspaper, "USA Today", with a circulation of 1.4 million. They also publish 42 weekly newspapers, own 16 radio and 9 TV stations, an advertising company and a popular questionnaire since. The list could go on. In recent years, Gannett has benn considerably aggressive in the newspaper market. A number of their daily newspapers have doubled circulation in a decade. The Company purchased "Family Weekly" (a Sunday supplement for 267 newspapers over 14 million copies), which was renamed to "US Week-End". She also bought the Evening News Association: 5 weekly newspapers, 2 radio stations and 5 TV stations.

Second place in terms of total circulation of daily newspapers is taken by "Night-ReaderNewspapers" that owns 32 dailies with a circulation of over 3.6 million and 6 weekly newspapers. The company's largest newspapers are "Detroit Free Press" (over 639,000 copies), "Philadelphia Inquirer" (494,000 copies) and "Miami Herald" (over 437,000 copies). The company also publishes a daily newspaper "Journal of Commerce and Commersional" (22,000 copies) has 4 TV stations and a paper factory.

Furthermore the "News House Newspapers" monopoly supports 26 daily newspapers with a total circulation of about 3 million. Her largest newspaper is "Cleveland Plane Dealer"(454,000 thousand copies). The company also owns weekly magazine "Parade" the largest weekly magazine circulation in the country at over 32.5 million copies, distributed as a Sunday supplement to 313 newspapers and the weekly "New-Yorker" (over 500,000 copies). In addition, News House owns "Conde Nast Magazines", a company that publishes wamens magazines, including "Vogue", "Mademoiselle" and "Glamour", the large publishing firm "Random House" as well as radio- and TV-stations.

The ten largest newspapers monopolies include: "Tribune Company" (7 daily newspapers with circulation of over 2.6 million, including "New York Daily News"—1.28 million copies and "Chicago Tribune"—758,000 copies); "Times Mirror" (6 daily newspapers with a circulation of over 2.6 million, including "Los Angeles Times"—over 1.1 million copies, "News Day"—624,000 copies and 5 magazines); "Dow Jones and Company" (23 daily newspapers with a circulation of over 2.5 million, including "Wall Street Journal"—the largest newspaper in the country with the highest circulation—nearly 2 million); "New York Times Company" (25 daily newspapers with a circulation of over 1.8 million including the leading "New York Times"—over 1 million copies, 7 weekly newspapers, and the magazine "Family Circle"—6.2 million copies); "Thomson Newspapers" (84 daily newspapers with a circulation of over 1.4 million copies, 4 weekly publications, 23 special magazines); "Hurst Corporation" (15 daily newspapers including "San Francisco Chronicle" —557,000 copies, "Los Angeles Herald Examiner"—285,000 copies, 40 weekly newspapers and 13 magazines including "Good Housekeeping"—5 million copies, "Red Book"—4 million copies, "Cosmopolitan"—2.9 million copies).

The leading newspaper monopolies also include "Capital Cities Communications" (which purchased ABC TV-Company in 1985), "Washington Post Company", and the corporations owned by Murdock, Scrips-Howard, Hart-Hanks, Cokes, Kopley, "Media General" and others. "Time Incorporated" occupies a leading place among magazine monopolies—a publisher of six magazines ("Time", "Life", "Fortune", "Sports Illustrated", "People", "Money") with a total circulation of over 13 million. "Time Incorporated" own a publishing house, cable TV systems, paper factories, etc. "Mk Grow-Hill" Concern is the largest publisher of business magazines in the world (over 60). One of its leading magazines is "Business Week" (over 875,000 copies) and the company also publishes text-books, directories and other literature.

"Readers Digest Association" publishes two magazines its monthly "Readers Digest" with a US circulation of 16.6 million and 39 foreign publications in 15 languages. Its entire, global circulation is over 28 million. Other large monopolic in magazine publishing are: "Try-Angle Publication" (2 publications including "TV Guide"—16.8 million, "Makkol Corporation" (4 magazines including a ladies' magazine "Makkols"—5.2 million copies), "Meredith" ("Better Homes and Gardens"—over 8 million copies), "Mk Fatten" Company (ladies' magazines including "True Story"—over 1.5 million copies), etc. The printing industry produces massive profits, and the largest newspaper-magazine monopolies possess a very solid place side by side with the leading industrial corporations of the country. Monopolies such as "Times Mirror", "Gannett Company", "Tribune Company", "Night Readers Newspapers", "Time Incorporated", "Mk Grow Hill", "New York Times Company", "Washington Post Company", "Dow Jones and Company", "Capita Cities Communications", "Meredith" enter the so-called "Club 500"—a list of the nation's leading corporations published by "Fortune" magazine every year.

The largest newspaper-magazine companies of Thomson, Merdock, Hurst, Gannett, "Dow Jones", "Time Incorporated", "Readers Digest Association", "Mk Grow-Hill", "New York Times Company", "Washington Post Company" bear an international and transnational character.

Daily newspapers occupy a leading role in country's system of newspaper printing. A majority of American daily newspapers (72%) are evening ones, however, their number has decreased and there is a crisis in the evening press conditioned by competition from TV, other newspapers and other factors. Evening newspapers have closed merged with morning ones or transferred into morning ones.

A specific characteristic of American newspapers is that they bears a mostly regional or local character. A majority of papers are distributed within the town or state where they are published. This is conditioned by historical development of newspaper printing in the US, the expense of supplying newspapers long distances and, mostly, by their dependence on local advertisements. Circulation figures of American newspapers are not high. The majority of the country's daily newspapers (1,417) possess a circulation of less than 50,000 copies. Only 35 newspapers have a circulation of 250,000 or more. Average circulation of a daily is 34,800 copies, and the number of newspaper copies per 1000 capita (282 copies in the USA) lags behind other leading capitalist countries.

In fact, until the late 1970s and early 1980s there weren't any national newspapers. Several such as "New York Times", "Washington Post", "Christian Science Monitor" and the financial "Wall-Street Journal" did distribute a small portion of their circulation beyond their state boundaries. Nowadays, with satellite communication in operation, a tendency towards creating a national newspaper press has developed "Wall-Street Journal" has become national (its 4 regional publications are printed in different states through satellite). "USA Today" (1.4 million copies) has been published in Washington since 1982. A national weekly edition of "Washington Post" started in 1984. "Wall-Street Journal" and "USA Today" are printed in Europe and Asia through satellite. They are becoming transnational and global newspapers, alongside the American "International Herald Tribune" published in Paris.

The concept "big press" includes large city newspapers—New York, Chicago, Los Angeles, Detroit, San Francisco, Philadelphia, Boston etc. In 1987, the largest newspaper circulations, apart from those already mentioned, were "New York Daily News" (1.28 million copies), "Los Angeles Times" (over 1.1 million), "New York Times" (over 1 million), "Chicago Tribune" (758,000 copies), "Detroit News" (678,000 copies), "Detroit Free Press" (639,000 copies),

"San-Francisco Chronicle" (557,000 copies), "Boston Globe" (500,000 copies) and others.

Suburban newspapers pose serious competition to the newspapers of big cities and towns. There are over 1,000 suburban newspapers with a total circulation of 13 million published across the country. The largest suburban newspaper in the USA is "News Day" of Long Island (624,000 copies) that competes successfully with the newspapers of New York.

In recent years free newspapers have developed widely. They are entirely on revenue from advertising and sent, by free post, as advertising materials. A part of them publishes nothing but advertisements, and another part publishes a very small quantity of the information. There are over 3,000 free newspapers in the country, with a circulation of 34 million.

Experts believe the future for the newspaper industry lies in an electronic newspaper. They believed that by the end of the 20th century, 40% of American families would read a newspaper on video terminal. However, the experiments carried out electronic newspaper format have revealed that it is not profitable, that the market is not yet ready for video text, and so the arena is very limited.

Press-syndicates exert considerable influence upon the activities of newspapers, especially local ones. There are private agencies specialised to supply various production needs to newspapers – such as articles, studies, comments, illustrations, full lines, women's pages, etc. There are over 350 press-syndicates in the country, and the largest ones distribute over 100 types of press production: The syndicated materials are published in hundreds of US and Canadian newspapers simultaneously. For instance, the words of J. Anderson, a political observer, are published by nearly 800 newspapers, advice by Ann Launders and Abby (Abigail Van Burin) are published in nearly 1,000 newspapers and the comics "Peanuts" and "Blonde"—in nearly 2,000 newspapers in the USA and Canada.

The country possesses a very strong and broad magazine press. The magazine reading audience is more differentiated than the newspaper one. This is connected to the fact that the majority of newspapers are general political press, and magazines (those of a general nature excluded) are various in character and so are instead for specific readers.

The 11,500 American magazines and journals have a total circulation that exceeds 350 million. Monthly publications prevail in the country's magazine press (they were 4,031). In the same year there were 1,984 quarterly publications, 1,400 weekly publications and 1,402 issued once every two months.

A specific character of magazines is that, in a contradiction to a more local and regional newspaper press of the majority the magazines are distributed across the nation. This conditions a large circulation of magazines than newspapers over 50 magazines have a circulation exceeding 1 million; six magazines boast a circulation that exceeds 10 million.

The American magazine market is characterised by a great number of various types of publications. A social differentiation conditions an availability of publications for the elite as and for the masses.

The most influential magazines are political weekly publications, so-called "magazines of news"- such as "Time" (4.8 million copies, with four main foreign editions—nearly 6 million copies), "News Week" (over 3 million copies, with three foreign editions – 3.5 million copies) and "US News and World Report" (2.2 million copies). The purpose of weekly publications is to sum up and interpret the news of the previous week for the interests of a "business-like" person. This "explanation" of the news is presented in the tendentious position of "information" magazines that in reality deal with news propaganda and interpretation according to its policy. Among the magazine-digests, "Readers Digest" stands out. It is a monthly publication of pocket size, re-printing articles from other publications and publishing its own as well. A giant of the information propaganda industry, circulation of the domestic edition is 16.6 million, which the 39 foreign editions make over 28 million copies. The magazine maintains a very skilfull balance of propaganda politics, diluting political articles with informative and entertaining articles.

Magazines have a large circulation Sunday newspaper supplements contain mostly entertaining pieces ("Parade"—32,5 million copies, "USA Week-end"—over 14 million copies), women's and housekeeping magazines ("Woman's Day", "Family Circle", "Better Homes and Gardens", "Good Housekeeping", "Lady's Home Journal"). Magazines for men, which, together with all materials of a bourgeois "mass culture" naturally relish sex, publish serious articles on political questions and works of literature ("Playboy", "Penthouse"). Entertaining, cheap magazines and comics also have a great circulation.

Among small publications, the most influential are the literary-political and the political-economic magazines ("Business Week", "Fortune", "Forbes"), magazines ("Atlantic", "Harpers", "New Yorker") and the magazines concerned with foreign policy ("Foreign Affairs", "Foreign Policy").

The magazines represent a wider range of political orientation within a bourgeois ideology that newspapers, from left-liberal to ultra-right. The viewpoints of different political groups are reflected in magazines of different opinions. As a rule, their circulation is not large, but their influence is on political processes is high. There is a small group of liberal magazines—"Nation", "Progressive", "New Republic", "Mother Jones". There is a wider group of right using magazines that includes "traditional" conservative editions ("National Review", "Human Events"), new conservatives ("Commentary", "Public Interest"), "new right" ("Conservative Digest") and the ultra-right ("New American", ex- "American Opinion").

Specialized periodicals are a very important component of the USA information set. The largest of them are business (industrial), religious, for ethnic groups, military and trade union press. An association of the USA business press unites over 2,800 publications with a total circulation of nearly 65 million. Pentagon publishes over 1,000 newspapers, nearly 400 magazines and different reports and statistics with a total circulation of over 12 million. The Catholic Church publishes over 400 editions and different Protestant Churches, over 1,500. 43 ethnic groups publish nearly 900 magazines with a total circulation of over 8 million ...

In this connection I suggest that newspaper industry should be considered as economic theory comprising two sections:

- production of newspapers as socially organized process (production of information values);
- production of readers' services—information services.

In line with the assumption mentioned above general functional and structural pattern should be:

- production of newspapers—information values;
- production of information services, assimilation of people's spare time with the aid of newspapers.

A) Productive forces oriented for creation of newspaper values:

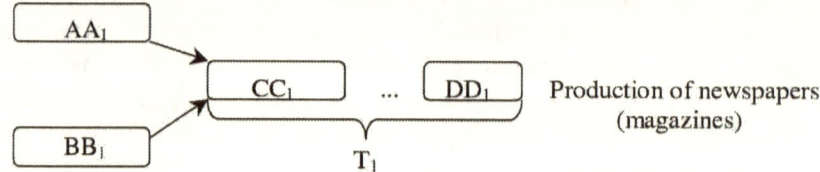

where
   $AA_1$—instruments of labor
   $BB_1$—subject of labor
   $CC_1$—labor resources

B) Productive forces of second kind oriented for creation of newspaper services:

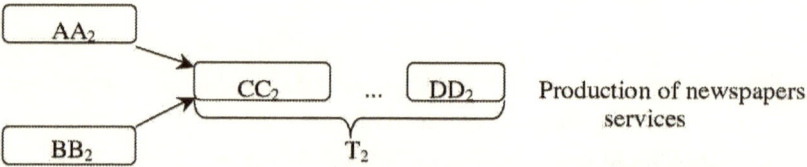

where
   $AA_2$—instruments of labor

   $BB_2$—subject of labor

   $CC_2$—labor resources

C) Complex productive forces of press industry:

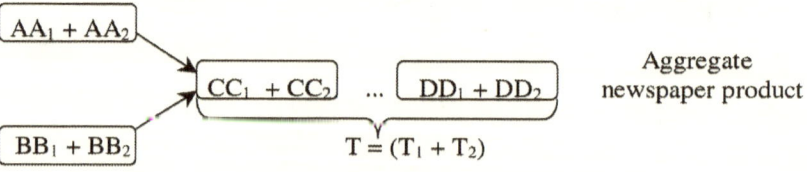

How does the movement of newspaper services and aggregate newspaper product occur in the economic space?

At first approach the movement of these specific values and services in the economic space can be represented as follows:

| Economic estimations of process of production | Economic estimations of process of distribution | Economic estimations of process of exchange | Economic estimations of process of consumption |
| --- | --- | --- | --- |
| Process of production of newspaper values | Process of distribution of newspaper values | Process of exchange of newspaper values | Process of consumption of newspaper values |
| Process of production of newspaper services | Process of distribution of newspaper services | Process of exchange of newspaper services | Process of consumption of newspaper services |
| Process of production of aggregate newspaper product | Process of distribution of aggregate newspaper product | Process of exchange of aggregate newspaper product | Process of consumption of aggregate newspaper product |

Everything that is framed by a dotted line is absent in the economic theory.

Our conception of the fourth branch of power will change considerably if we move away from traditional way of examining its problems and have an unusual look at it. For instance, by taking into account spare time of the population assimilated by the newspaper industry.

Until recently economic aspect of publishing activity has been investigated detachedly from such an economic component as spare time of the population assimilated by the newspapers.

This resource has been ignored in the theory as one of the resultant components of the newspaper industry.

## 2.  PROBLEMS OF ASSIMILATION OF THE ASTP RESOURCE BY THE FOURTH BRANCH OF POWER

In my research of this group of problems I proceed from the basis that an assimilated resource of the population's spare time is a guideline for their activities. Nikulin V.V. and Strunina O.N. express a similar thought: «we chose the time spent on reading newspapers as a measuring unit of consuming newspaper information. The time of consumption is individual and depends on education and personal habits. But these differences fade while investigating the aggregate information. Time can be used as an average indicator».

Hence, we suggest that «time» or period of consumption of newspaper services should be used as one of the absolute indicators of the newspaper industry activity. This unit of measure of the activity results is natural. Newspaper services can not be measured by meters or kilograms. Time of consumption of newspaper services is the only natural measure. The newspaper industry activity is aimed at assimilated spare time of population resource. Assimilated newspaper services resource represents, to my opinion, «the measure of their consumption».

This logic is not erroneous, it is correct in itself since economic advances of the newspaper industry are directly linked with the people's spare time assimilated by it.

I offer to investigate the movement of newspapers (magazines) in the economic space taking into account spare time of the population resource, i.e. the human resource with the time component. The resource, assimilation of which the newspaper industry is aimed at. The movement of newspapers (magazines) with the $A_{STP}$ resource in the economic space is taking place as follows:

| Economic criteria of process of production | Economic criteria of process of distribution | Economic criteria of process of exchange | Economic criteria of process of consumption |
|---|---|---|---|
| Newspapers, magazines | Newspapers, magazines | Newspapers, magazines | Newspapers, magazines |
| Newspaper services including $A_{STP}$ | Newspaper services including $A_{STP}$ | Newspaper services including $A_{STP}$ | Newspaper services including $A_{STP}$ |
| Aggregate newspaper product including $A_{STP}$ | Aggregate newspaper product including $A_{STP}$ | Aggregate newspaper product including $A_{STP}$ | Aggregate newspaper product including $A_{STP}$ |

| Economic indicators of process of production | Economic indicators of process of distribution | Economic indicators of process of exchange | Economic indicators of process of consumption |
|---|---|---|---|
| Newspapers, magazines | Newspapers, magazines | Newspapers, magazines | Newspapers, magazines |
| Newspaper services including $A_{STP}$ | Newspaper services including $A_{STP}$ | Newspaper services including $A_{STP}$ | Newspaper services including $A_{STP}$ |
| Aggregate newspaper product including $A_{STP}$ | Aggregate newspaper product including $A_{STP}$ | Aggregate newspaper product including $A_{STP}$ | Aggregate newspaper product including $A_{STP}$ |

| Process of production | Process of distribution | Process of exchange | Process of consumption |
| --- | --- | --- | --- |
| Newspapers, magazines | Newspapers, magazines | Newspapers, magazines | Newspapers, magazines |
| Newspaper services including $A_{STP}$ | Newspaper services including $A_{STP}$ | Newspaper services including $A_{STP}$ | Newspaper services including $A_{STP}$ |
| Aggregate newspaper product including $A_{STP}$ | Aggregate newspaper product including $A_{STP}$ | Aggregate newspaper product including $A_{STP}$ | Aggregate newspaper product including $A_{STP}$ |

| Process of production | Process of distribution | Process of exchange | Process of consumption |
| --- | --- | --- | --- |
| Newspapers, magazines | Newspapers, magazines | Newspapers, magazines | Newspapers, magazines |
| Newspaper services including $A_{STP}$ | Newspaper services including $A_{STP}$ | Newspaper services including $A_{STP}$ | Newspaper services including $A_{STP}$ |
| Aggregate newspaper product including $A_{STP}$ | Aggregate newspaper product including $A_{STP}$ | Aggregate newspaper product including $A_{STP}$ | Aggregate newspaper product including $A_{STP}$ |

At every stage of movement of the fourth power values and services economic estimates, criteria and indicators should be available.

## 2. Services of the fourth power

| Branches | Volume of the fourth power services (production use) | | | | Volume of the fourth power services (non-production use) | | | | Aggregate volume of services of the fourth power | | | | | | |
|---|---|---|---|---|---|---|---|---|---|---|---|---|---|---|---|
| | № 1 | № 2 | № 3 | № 4 | № 5 | № 6 | № 7 | № 8 | № 9 | № 10 | № 11 | № 12 | Estimations | Criteria | Indicators |
| | | | | | | | | | | | | | Estimations | Criteria | Indicators |
| | | | | | | | | | | | | | Estimations | Criteria | Indicators |
| | | | | | | | | | | | | | Estimations | Criteria | Indicators |
| | | | | | | | | | | | | | Estimations | Criteria | Indicators |
| I branch | Production needs in services of the fourth power (estimation) $C_2 + V_2^P i + m_2^P j$ | | | | | | | | | | | | Estimations | Criteria | Indicators |
| | | | | | | | | | | | | | Estimations | Criteria | Indicators |
| | | | | | | | | | | | | | Estimations | Criteria | Indicators |
| | | | | | | | | | | | | | Estimations | Criteria | Indicators |
| II branch | Non-production needs in services of the fourth power (estimation) $V_2^{NP} i + m_2^{NP} j + A_{STPD}$ | | | | | | | | | | | | Estimations | Criteria | Indicators |
| | | | | | | | | | | | | | Estimations | Criteria | Indicators |
| | | | | | | | | | | | | | Estimations | Criteria | Indicators |
| | | | | | | | | | | | | | Estimations | Criteria | Indicators |
| III branch | Complex needs in services of the fourth power (estimation) | | | | | | | | | | | | Estimations | Criteria | Indicators |
| | | | | | | | | | | | | | Estimations | Criteria | Indicators |

## E.  PRODUCTION AND NON-PRODUCTION CHARACTER OF CONSUMPTION OF FORTH POWER VALUES AND SERVICES

Needs of the fourth branch of power are being met along two interopposed planes:

- part of the fourth power needs have production character;
- part of the fourth power needs are of non-production character.

In general the structure of production needs of values and services of the fourth branch of power is as follows:

a) production needs of values of the fourth power;

b) production needs of services of the fourth power;

c) production needs of aggregate product of the fourth power.

Non-production character of meeting educational needs has the following structure:

a) non-production needs of the fourth power values;

b) non-production needs of the fourth power services;

c) non-production needs of aggregate product of the fourth power.

The above mentioned can be interpreted by the following logical table:

| | Production consumption | Non-production consumption | Aggregate consumption |
|---|---|---|---|
| 1. | Values of the fourth power | Values of the fourth power | Values of the fourth power |
| 2. | Services of the fourth power | Services of the fourth power | Services of the fourth power |
| 3. | Aggregate product of the fourth power | Aggregate product of the fourth power | Aggregate product of the fourth power |

Non-production consumption

1)  $C_1 + V_1^P i + V_1^{NP} i + m_1^P j + m_1^{NP} j = R_1$

Production consumption

Non-production consumption

2)  $C_2 + V_2^P i + V_2^{NP} i + m_2^P j + m_2^{NP} j + A_{STP} d = R_2$

Production consumption

## 1. Values of the fourth power branch

| Branches | Volume of values of the fourth power branch (production use) | | | | Volume of values of the fourth power branch (non-production use) | | | | Aggregate volume of values of the fourth power branch | | | | | | |
|---|---|---|---|---|---|---|---|---|---|---|---|---|---|---|---|
| | № 1 | № 2 | № 3 | № 4 | № 5 | № 6 | № 7 | № 8 | № 9 | № 10 | № 11 | № 12 | Estimations | Criteria | Indicators |
| I branch | Production needs in values of the fourth power branch (estimation) $C_i + V^P_1 i + m^P_1 j$ | | | | | | | | | | | | Estimations | Criteria | Indicators |
| | | | | | | | | | | | | | Estimations | Criteria | Indicators |
| | | | | | | | | | | | | | Estimations | Criteria | Indicators |
| | | | | | | | | | | | | | Estimations | Criteria | Indicators |
| II branch | | | | | Non-production needs in values of the fourth power branch (estimation) $V^{NP}_1 i + m^{NP}_1 j$ | | | | | | | | Estimations | Criteria | Indicators |
| | | | | | | | | | | | | | Estimations | Criteria | Indicators |
| | | | | | | | | | | | | | Estimations | Criteria | Indicators |
| | | | | | | | | | | | | | Estimations | Criteria | Indicators |
| III branch | | | | | | | | | Complex production needs in values of the fourth power branch (estimation) | | | | Estimations | Criteria | Indicators |
| | | | | | | | | | | | | | Estimations | Criteria | Indicators |

## 2. Services of the fourth power branch

| Branches | Volume of the fourth power branch services (production use) | | | | Volume of the fourth power branch services (non-production use) | | | | Aggregate volume of services of the fourth power branch | | | | Estimations | Criteria | Indicators |
|---|---|---|---|---|---|---|---|---|---|---|---|---|---|---|---|
| | № 1 | № 2 | № 3 | № 4 | № 5 | № 6 | № 7 | № 8 | № 9 | № 10 | № 11 | № 12 | | | |
| I branch — Production needs in services of the fourth power branch (estimation) $C_2 + V_2^{P}i + m_2^{P}j$ | | | | | | | | | | | | | Estimations | Criteria | Indicators |
| | | | | | | | | | | | | | Estimations | Criteria | Indicators |
| | | | | | | | | | | | | | Estimations | Criteria | Indicators |
| | | | | | | | | | | | | | Estimations | Criteria | Indicators |
| | | | | | | | | | | | | | Estimations | Criteria | Indicators |
| II branch — Non-production needs in services of the fourth power branch (estimation) $V_2^{NP}i + m_2^{NP}j + A_{smp d}$ | | | | | | | | | | | | | Estimations | Criteria | Indicators |
| | | | | | | | | | | | | | Estimations | Criteria | Indicators |
| | | | | | | | | | | | | | Estimations | Criteria | Indicators |
| III branch — Complex needs in services of the fourth power branch (estimation) | | | | | | | | | | | | | Estimations | Criteria | Indicators |
| | | | | | | | | | | | | | Estimations | Criteria | Indicators |

I)   INDICATORS OF LONG-TERM PROVISION OF VALUES AND
     SERVICES OF THE FOURTH POWER BRANCH

   A.    STRUCTURE OF LONG-TERM
         NEEDS OF VALUES OF THE FOURTH POWER BRANCH

**Thesis**    An increment ($\Delta$) of the volume of production needs in values of the fourth power branch

**Antithesis**   An increment ($\Delta$) of the volume of non-production needs in values of the fourth power branch

**Synthesis**   An increment ($\Delta$) of the volume of aggregate needs (both production and non-production character) in values of the fourth power branch

   AA.    INDICATOR OF LONG-TERM
          «PROVISION OF THE FOURTH POWER BRANCH» (OF A
          PRODUCTION PURPOSE)

**Thesis**    Increment ($\Delta$) of the volume of values of fourth power branch production purpose ($\Delta$V-VAL-P)

**Antithesis**   Increment ($\Delta$) production needs in values of the fourth power branch

$$\frac{(\Delta V\text{-}VAL\text{-}P)}{\text{Increment } (\Delta) \text{ production needs in values of the fourth power branch}}$$

**Synthesis**    —————————————————    —indicator

   AAA.    INDICATOR OF LONG-TERM
           «PROVISION OF THE FOURTH POWER BRANCH»
           (OF A NON-PRODUCTION PURPOSE)

**Thesis**    Increment ($\Delta$) of the volume values of the fourth power branch non-production purpose ($\Delta$V-VAL-NP)

**Antithesis**   Increment ($\Delta$) non-production needs in values of the fourth power branch

$$(\Delta V\text{-}VAL\text{-}NP)$$

Synthesis ——————————————— —indicator

Increment ($\Delta$) non-production

needs in values of the fourth power branch

| SYSTEM OF INDICATORS OF LONG-TERM OF THE FOURTH POWER BRANCH AS AGAINST FUNCTIONAL INDICATION | | | |
|---|---|---|---|
| | THESIS | ANTITHESIS | SYNTHESIS |
| **THESIS** Dialectical structure of long term aggregate values of the fourth power branch | An increment ($\Delta$) of the volume of values of the fourth power branch ($\Delta$VVP) for production purpose | An increment ($\Delta$) of the volume values of the fourth power branch non-production purpose ($\Delta$V-VAL-NP) | An increment ($\Delta$) of the volume of the aggregate values of the fourth power branch for production and non-production purpose |
| **ANTITHESIS** Dialectical structure of long-term needs of the fourth power branch | An increment ($\Delta$) of production needs in values of the fourth power branch ($\Delta$VVN) | An increment ($\Delta$) of non-production needs in values of the fourth power branch | An increment ($\Delta$) of aggregate needs in values of the fourth power branch of production and non-production purpose |
| **SYNTHESIS** Dialectical structure of indicator of long-term provision of the fourth power branch | An increment ($\Delta$) of the volume of values of the fourth power branch ($\Delta$VVP) for production purpose  An increment ($\Delta$) of production needs of values of the fourth power branch ($\Delta$VVN) | An increment ($\Delta$) of the volume values of the fourth power branch non-production purpose ($\Delta$VED-VAL-NP)  An increment ($\Delta$) of non-production needs in values of the fourth power branch | An increment ($\Delta$) of the aggregate values of the fourth power branch for production and non-production consumption  An increment ($\Delta$) of aggregate needs of the fourth power branch production and non-production purpose |

# CHAPTER 2

# THE FIFTH BRANCH OF POWER – RADIO SPHERE

## 1. SPECIFICATION OF RADIO SPHERE AS AN ECONOMIC SYSTEM

A centenary has passed since the invention of radio. Over these years broadcast-ing has been transformed into a huge economic system. In the USA alone there are about 3000 FM and about 1000 of other kinds of public Radio Broadcasting stations. People have about 500 mln. radio receivers at their disposal. Broadcasting has its own sector of services, expenditure and specific results.

How to establish economic purpose of radio broadcast if its results are being put on the air, i.e. into space?

The answer to this question can be given provided we consider broadcasting as an economic system.

Broadcasting comprises two forms of activities:

a) creation of radio reporting, etc. in a material form;

b) application of radio materials for the creation of broadcasting services.

Proceeding from that, expenses of the broadcasting sphere can be classified as:

a) group of expenses I—expenses connected to the creation of radio reports, interviews;

b) group of expenses II—expenses related to putting on the air, creating radio services (information services).

I add up these activities into a system on the grounds that they functionally sup-plement each other.

Aggregate production capacity of «Radio broadcasting».

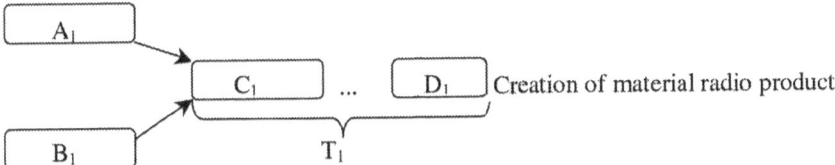

where
    $A_1$—instruments of labor
    $B_1$—subject of labor
    $C_1$—labor resources

B) Productive forces of second kind oriented for creation of radio services:

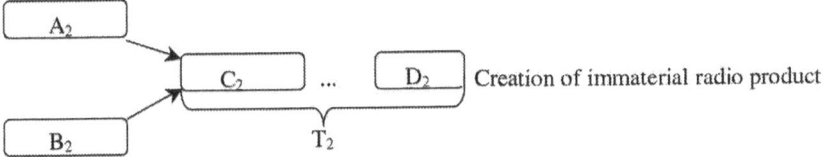

where
    $A_2$—instruments of labor
    $B_2$—subject of labor
    $C_2$—labor resources

C) Complex productive forces of radio sphere:

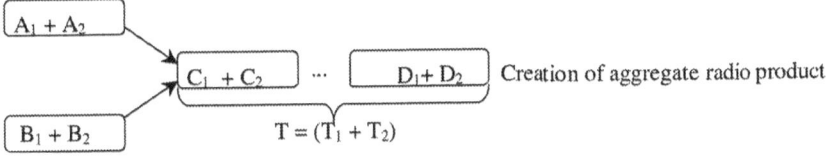

The movement of these radio values and services in the economic space can be interpreted as:

## TABLE 1 THE SYSTEM OF ECONOMIC ESTIMATES

| Process of production | Process of distribution | Process of exchange | Process of consumption |
|---|---|---|---|
| Material radio stuff | Material radio stuff | Material radio stuff | Material radio stuff |
| Radio services | Radio services | Radio services | Radio services |
| Aggregate radio product | Aggregate radio product | Aggregate radio product | Aggregate radio product |

## I.  ESTIMATION OF MOVEMENT OF RADIO VALUES AND SERVICES IN ECONOMIC SPACE

1.  I proceed from the fact that material radio product, radio service and aggregate radio product possess necessary economic qualities to enable them to move in the economic space.

Absence of such properties would reduce their movement to zero.

2.  It is worth pointing out that Radio Broadcasting services have their own peculiarities of creation, distribution and consumption.

Within one time interval the following is taking place, i.e.

a) Radio Broadcasting has come to an end—distribution of radio services in time and space has also ended;

b) Radio Broadcasting ends together with the population's involvement in the process of radio services consumption.

The above mentioned peculiarities can be graphically represented as follows:

Time to create radio services
Time to distribute radio services
Time to consume radio services

Time interval—T

Relations of «exchange» associated with the radio sphere do not always coincide with the process of production, consumption and distribution of radio services.

In some cases there is monthly budgetary financing of Radio Broadcasting, in other ones prepayment for advertising services.

Until now radio sphere has been estimated with no account of spare time of the population resource assimilated by radio services—$A_{STP}$. This negative point adversely affects quality of estimation of production, distribution, exchange and consumption of radio values and services.

## TABLE 2 THE SYSTEM OF ECONOMIC ESTIMATES

| | Economic estimation of production | Economic estimation of distribution | Economic estimation of exchange | Economic estimation of consumption |
|---|---|---|---|---|
| A. | Economic estimation of production of material radio stuff | Economic estimation of distribution of material radio stuff | Economic estimation of exchange of material radio stuff | Economic estimation of consumption of material radio stuff |
| B. | Economic estimation of production of radio services without $A_{STP}$ | Economic estimation of distribution of radio services without $A_{STP}$ | Economic estimation of exchange radio services without $A_{STP}$ | Economic estimation of consumption of radio services without $A_{STP}$ |
| C. | Economic estimation of production of aggregate radio product without $A_{STP}$ | Economic estimation of distribution of aggregate radio product without $A_{STP}$ | Economic estimation of exchange of aggregate radio product without $A_{STP}$ | Economic estimation of consumption of aggregate radio product without $A_{STP}$ |

At present estimation of the activity results in this branch is made by the amount of expenses related to its functioning. Incomes from advertisement should be added to these expenses. In such a way the cost of amount of broadcasting services provided for the population is being established. However, we have to cope with considerable number of problems here. For example, if the broadcasting services are oriented on the man – as a radio listener – the latter, as a «subject of labor» be included in the cost of radio services.

However, one will not be able to find in any of the textbooks such a method of calculation of broadcasting services together with this specific subject of labor.

Spare time of the population resource has always been the asset of the society. «Spare time of the population» category is not included in the GDP.

## A. ECONOMIC ESTIMATE OF RADIO BROADCASTING SERVICES

For a hundred years, spare time of human resource has not been taken into account in radio broadcasting. For this reason cost value of the created product is being brought down. In our case by the amount of «subject of labor»—spare time of population resource assimilated by the radio broadcasting services.

This is a logical mistake which has to be corrected. Cost value of the radio broadcasting services will be recorded as:

$$C + V + A^R_{STP} = Z$$

where

C—past labor expenses connected to exploitation of radio broadcasting techniques;

V—direct labor expenses associated with the production of radio broadcasting services;

$A^R_{STP}$—cost value of the spare time of the population resource assimilated by the radio broadcasting services (but not paid by the consumer).

The nature of origin of the a, b, $A_{STP}$ resources is heterogeneous. This circumstance makes it possible to place resources involved in the broadcasting on different axes (X, Y, Z), provided that three-dimensional coordinates are used.

Radio broadcasting service will be recorded as:

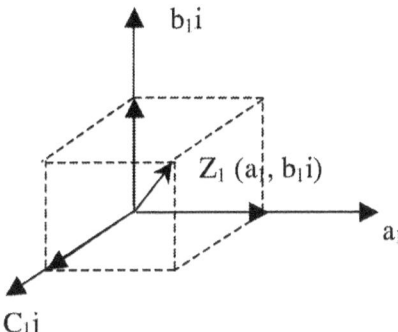

where

a$_1$—cost of the created material radio stuff in a year;

b$_1$i—direct labor expenses connected to transmission of radio services;

C$_1$j—cost value of the assimilated spare time of the population resource, involved in the process of creating radio-services.

Aggregate vector R will be written as follows:

$$R = a_1 + b_1i + C_1j$$

This vector reveals the aggregate cost of the radio product, created in a year.

Such a form of recording economic results of radio broadcasting is very handy. Reduction of the number of radio listeners will cause contraction of Cj – vector, and consequently of the aggregate R-vector value.

Increase of the number of radio listeners cause extension of Cj – vector value and respectively of R-vector value.

Such a form of recording of radio broadcasting services as a complex number suggests application of specific operations of addition, subtraction, multiplication, division, etc.

Operations 1 Addition

Operations 2 Subtraction

Operations 3 Multiplication

Operations 4 Division

The usage of complex numbers in economic estimations of radio services makes it possible to examine economic space occupied by the radio in a different way.

### TABLE 3 THE SYSTEM OF ECONOMIC ESTIMATES

| | Economic estimation of production | Economic estimation of distribution | Economic estimation of exchange | Economic estimation of consumption |
|---|---|---|---|---|
| A. | Economic estimation of production of material radio stuff | Economic estimation of distribution of material radio stuff | Economic estimation of exchange of material radio stuff | Economic estimation of consumption of material radio stuff |
| B. | Economic estimation of production of radio services including $A_{STP}$ | Economic estimation of distribution of radio services including $A_{STP}$ | Economic estimation of exchange of radio services including $A_{STP}$ | Economic estimation of consumption of radio services including $A_{STP}$ |
| C. | Economic estimation of production of aggregate radio product including $A_{STP}$ | Economic estimation of distribution of aggregate radio product including $A_{STP}$ | Economic estimation of exchange of aggregate radio product including $A_{STP}$ | Economic estimation of consumption of aggregate radio product including $A_{STP}$ |

A) Economic estimate of material radio stuff.

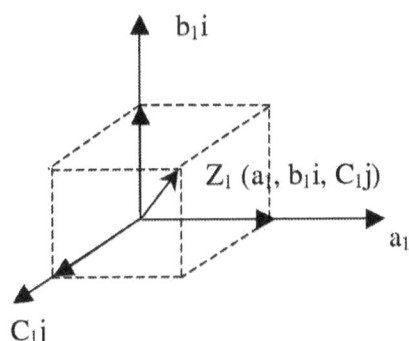

, where

    $C_1$—past labor expenses on creating Radio values;

    $V_1 i$—direct labor expenses on creating Radio values;

    $m_1 j$—incomes received from creating Radio values.

B) Economic estimates of radio services including $A_{STP}$.

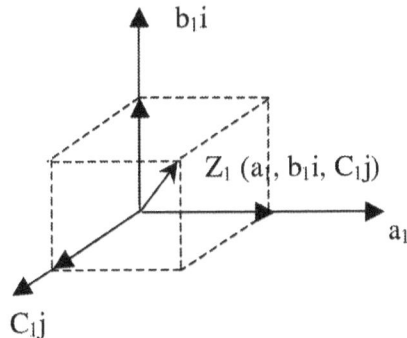

, where

    $C_2$—past labor expenses on creating Radio services;

    $V_2 i$—direct labor expenses on creating Radio services;

    $m_2 j$—incomes received from creating Radio services.

C) Economic estimates of aggregate radio product including $A_{STP}$.

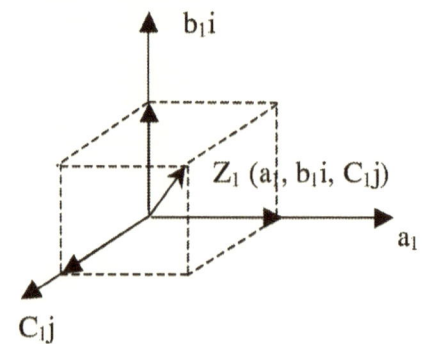

, where

a = $C_1$ + $C_2$—aggregate past labor expenses on creating Radio product;

bi = $V_1i$ + $V_2i$—aggregate direct labor expenses on creating Radio product;

Cj = $m_1j$ + $m_2j$—aggregate incomes received from creating Radio product.

If we subtract the first option of estimates from the second option of estimates of movement of radio values and services, we shall receive a system of errors in estimating the movement of radio values and services in economic space.

| | Errors in estimates of production | Errors in estimates of distribution | Errors in estimates of exchange | Errors in estimates of consumption |
|---|---|---|---|---|
| **A.** | Material radio stuff | Material radio stuff | Material radio stuff | Material radio stuff |
| **B.** | $\Delta_{21}$—errors | $\Delta_{22}$—errors | $\Delta_{23}$—errors | $\Delta_{24}$—errors |
| **C.** | $\Delta_{31}$—errors | $\Delta_{32}$—errors | $\Delta_{33}$—errors | $\Delta_{34}$—errors |

Hence, we have received a matrix of errors which needs to be corrected:

First, it is necessary to include ASTP resource into the radio services cost;

Second, to use operations with matrices applying complex numbers.

Informational services exist only at the moment of their creation, e.g. at a concert, in the cinema theatre, at a lecture, etc. The finale chords of the orchestra, the end of the film ultimate the creation of the informational service. In other terms, informational services commence, exist and promptly disappear.

They may be compared with flickering stars. Now they flash, now fade and disappear.

According to elementary logic of calculation of intellectual services it would be appropriate to apply numbers invented for non-standard situations. They are called imaginary ones and represent the whole class of such complex numbers.

$$Z = a + bi$$

I suggest to use complex numbers and corresponding operational system in dealing with the intellectual sphere economy.

There is not any motivation why we shall reject that group of numbers which would enhance the quality of economic calculations.

Complex numbers should be widely used keeping in mind though that mathematical operations of addition, subtraction, multiplication and division with them are different from the ones we are accustomed to.

a) addition of complex numbers;

$$z_1 + z_2 = (a_1 + b_1 i) + (a_2 + b_2 i) = (a_1 + a_2) + (b_1 i + b_2 i)$$

b) subtraction of complex numbers;

$$z_1 - z_2 = (a_1 + b_1 i) - (a_2 + b_2 i) = (a_1 - a_2) + (b_1 i - b_2 i)$$

c) multiplication of complex numbers;

$$z_1 z_2 = (a_1 + b_1 i) \times (a_2 + b_2 i) = a_1 a_2 + a_1 b_2 i + a_2 b_1 i + b_1 b_2 i^2 = a_1 a_2 + a_1 b_2 i +$$
$$+ a_2 b_1 i - b_1 b_2 = (a_1 a_2 - b_1 b_2) + (a_1 b_2 + a_2 b_1) i$$

d) division of complex numbers.

$$\frac{z_1}{z_2} = \frac{a_1 a_2 + b_1 b_2}{a_2^2 + b_2^2} + \frac{(a_2 b_1 - a_1 b_2)i}{a_2^2 + b_2^2}$$

The usage of complex numbers in economic calculations facilitates examination of things which were not liable to be taken into account due to the above mentioned reason.

These formulas are applicable for complex numbers. It is a specific arithmetic's with complex numbers and we shall not avoid operating it. In other words, it is the branch of theory which until recently has not been used in managing economic problems of broadcasting.

# 1. Values of the fifth power branch

| Branches | Volume of values of the fifth power branch (production use) | | | | Volume of values of the fifth power branch (non-production use) | | | | Aggregate volume of values of the fifth power branch | | | | | Estimations | Criteria | Indicators |
|---|---|---|---|---|---|---|---|---|---|---|---|---|---|---|---|---|
| | № 1 | № 2 | № 3 | № 4 | № 5 | № 6 | № 7 | № 8 | № 9 | № 10 | № 11 | № 12 | | | | |
| | | | | | | | | | | | | | | Estimations | Criteria | Indicators |
| | | | | | | | | | | | | | | Estimations | Criteria | Indicators |
| | | | | | | | | | | | | | | Estimations | Criteria | Indicators |
| | | | | | | | | | | | | | | Estimations | Criteria | Indicators |
| I branch | Production needs in values of the fifth power branch (estimation) $C_1 + V_1{}^{P}{}_i + m_1{}^{P}{}_j$ | | | | | | | | | | | | | Estimations | Criteria | Indicators |
| | | | | | | | | | | | | | | Estimations | Criteria | Indicators |
| | | | | | | | | | | | | | | Estimations | Criteria | Indicators |
| | | | | | | | | | | | | | | Estimations | Criteria | Indicators |
| II branch | Non-production needs in values of the fifth power branch (estimation) $V_1{}^{NP}{}_i + m_1{}^{NP}{}_j$ | | | | | | | | | | | | | Estimations | Criteria | Indicators |
| | | | | | | | | | | | | | | Estimations | Criteria | Indicators |
| | | | | | | | | | | | | | | Estimations | Criteria | Indicators |
| | | | | | | | | | | | | | | Estimations | Criteria | Indicators |
| III branch | Complex production needs in values of the fifth power branch (estimation) | | | | | | | | | | | | | Estimations | Criteria | Indicators |
| | | | | | | | | | | | | | | Estimations | Criteria | Indicators |

## 2. Services of the fifth power branch

| Branches | Volume of the fifth power branch services (production use) | | | | Volume of the fifth power branch services (non-production use) | | | | Aggregate volume of services of the fifth power branch | | | | Estimations | Criteria | Indicators |
|---|---|---|---|---|---|---|---|---|---|---|---|---|---|---|---|
| | № 1 | № 2 | № 3 | № 4 | № 5 | № 6 | № 7 | № 8 | № 9 | № 10 | № 11 | № 12 | | | |
| I branch — Production needs in services of the fifth power branch (estimation) $C_2 + V_2^{P_i} i + m_2^{P_j} j$ | | | | | | | | | | | | | Estimations | Criteria | Indicators |
| | | | | | | | | | | | | | Estimations | Criteria | Indicators |
| | | | | | | | | | | | | | Estimations | Criteria | Indicators |
| | | | | | | | | | | | | | Estimations | Criteria | Indicators |
| II branch — Non-production needs in services of the fifth power branch (estimation) $V_2^{NP_i} i + m_2^{NP_j} j + A_{synd}$ | | | | | | | | | | | | | Estimations | Criteria | Indicators |
| | | | | | | | | | | | | | Estimations | Criteria | Indicators |
| | | | | | | | | | | | | | Estimations | Criteria | Indicators |
| | | | | | | | | | | | | | Estimations | Criteria | Indicators |
| III branch — Complex needs in services of the fifth power branch (estimation) | | | | | | | | | | | | | Estimations | Criteria | Indicators |
| | | | | | | | | | | | | | Estimations | Criteria | Indicators |

I)  INDICATORS OF LONG-TERM PROVISION OF VALUES AND SERVICES OF THE FIFTH POWER BRANCH

A.  STRUCTURE OF LONG-TERM NEEDS OF VALUES OF THE FIFTH POWER BRANCH

**Thesis**      An increment ($\Delta$) of the volume of production needs in values of the fifth power branch

**Antithesis**  An increment ($\Delta$) of the volume of non-production needs in values of the fifth power branch

**Synthesis**   An increment ($\Delta$) of the volume of aggregate needs (both production and non-production character) in values of the fifth power branch

AA.  INDICATOR OF LONG-TERM «PROVISION OF THE FIFTH POWER BRANCH» (OF A PRODUCTION PURPOSE)

**Thesis**      Increment ($\Delta$) of the volume of values of fifth power branch production purpose ($\Delta$V-VAL-P)

**Antithesis**  Increment ($\Delta$) production needs in values of the fifth power branch

**Synthesis**   $$\frac{(\Delta\text{V-VAL-P})}{\text{Increment } (\Delta) \text{ production needs}} \text{ - indicator}$$
in values of the fifth power branch

AAA.  INDICATOR OF LONG-TERM «PROVISION OF THE FIFTH POWER BRANCH» (OF A NON-PRODUCTION PURPOSE)

**Thesis**      Increment ($\Delta$) of the volume values of the fifth power branch non-production purpose ($\Delta$V-VAL-NP)

**Antithesis**  Increment ($\Delta$) non-production needs in values of the fifth power branch

$$\text{Synthesis} \quad \frac{(\Delta V\text{-VAL-NP})}{\text{Increment } (\Delta) \text{ non-production}} \text{ - indicator}$$

needs in values of the fifth power branch

| SYSTEM OF INDICATORS OF LONG-TERM OF THE FIFTH POWER BRANCH AS AGAINST FUNCTIONAL INDICATION | | | |
|---|---|---|---|
| | **THESIS** | **ANTITHESIS** | **SYNTHESIS** |
| **THESIS** Dialectical structure of long term aggregate values of the fifth power branch | An increment $(\Delta)$ of the volume of values of the fifth power branch $(\Delta VVP)$ for production purpose | An increment $(\Delta)$ of the volume values of the fifth power branch non-production purpose $(\Delta V\text{-VAL-NP})$ | An increment $(\Delta)$ of the volume of the aggregate values of the fifth power branch for production and non-production purpose |
| **ANTITHESIS** Dialectical structure of long-term needs of the fifth power branch | An increment $(\Delta)$ of production needs in values of the fifth power branch $(\Delta VVN)$ | An increment $(\Delta)$ of non-production needs in values of the fifth power branch | An increment $(\Delta)$ of aggregate needs in values of the fifth power branch of production and non-production purpose |
| **SYNTHESIS** Dialectical structure of indicator of long-term provision of the fifth power branch | An increment $(\Delta)$ of the volume of values of the fifth power branch $(\Delta VVP)$ for production purpose <br><br> An increment $(\Delta)$ of production needs of values of the fifth power branch $(\Delta VVN)$ | An increment $(\Delta)$ of the volume values of the fifth power branch non-production purpose $(\Delta VED\text{-VAL-NP})$ <br><br> An increment $(\Delta)$ of non-production needs in values of the fifth power branch | An increment $(\Delta)$ of the aggregate values of the fifth power branch for production and non-production consumption <br> An increment $(\Delta)$ of aggregate needs of the fifth power branch production and non-production purpose |

# CHAPTER 3

# THE SIXTH BRANCH OF POWER—TELEVISION SPHERE

## 1) TELEVISION SPHERE AS AN ECONOMIC SYSTEM

It is still difficult to visualize the nature of movement of resources within this sphere. What do the movement patterns in the TV sphere look like?

What is the essence of the aggregate television product? How do the separate parts of the aggregate TV product move?

«Television» is the largest branch of the intellectual sphere judging by the number of people benefiting from its services. In European countries alone about 200 mln. people gather at TV screens every Saturday and Sunday. The amount of involvement of the human resource into the TV services assimilated in spare time can hardly be compared with any of the human streams of resources.[14]

A) Productive forces oriented for creation of television values:

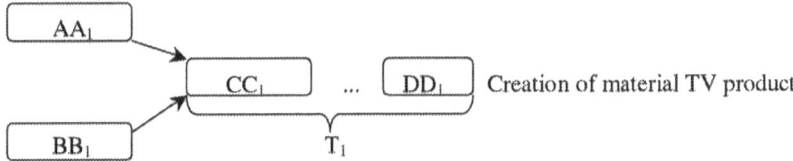

where
  $AA_1$—instruments of labor
  $BB_1$—subject of labor
  $CC_1$—labor resources

---

14    The above scheme allows to bring some order into the classification of expenses.
Group of expenses I—expenses related to the creation of material information values.
Group of expenses II—expenses related to telecast, transmission, creation of TV services.

B) Productive forces of second kind oriented for creation of television services:

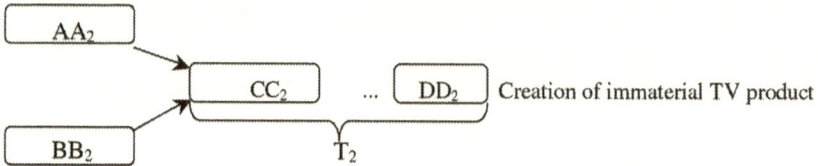

where

AA$_2$—instruments of labor

BB$_2$—subject of labor

CC$_2$—labor resources

C) Complex productive forces of television sphere:

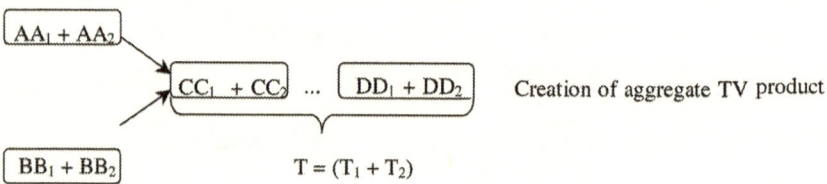

1. Television values can be introduced in a three-dimensional space as:

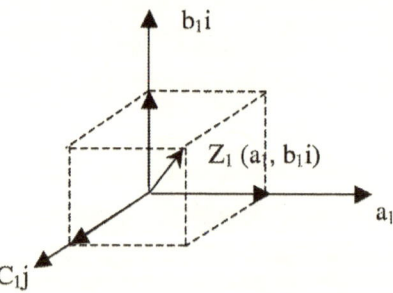

where    a$_1$—past labor expenses connected with production of television values;

b$_1$i—direct labor expenses connected with production of television values;

C$_1$j—incomes from creating television values.

2. Television service can be introduced in the three-dimensional space can be shown as:

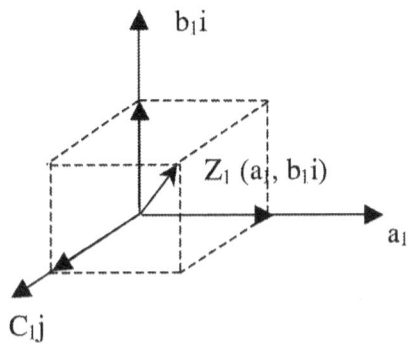

where  $a_1$—past labor expenses connected with production of television services;

$b_1 i$—direct labor expenses connected with production of television services;

$C_1 j$— assimilated $A_{STP}$ resource.

3. Formulized version of aggregate television product will be recorded as follows:

**Thesis**      Television production created in Division I (material form)

$$C_1 + V_1 i + m_1 j = Z_1$$

**Antithesis**  Television production created in Division II (service form)

$$C_2 + V_2 i + m_2 j + A_{STP} k = Z_2$$

**Synthesis**  Aggregate television production created in Divisions I & II

$$(C_1 + C_2) + (V_1 + V_2)i + (m_1 + m_2)j + A_{STP} k = Z_3$$

, where

$C_I$—expenses of past labor connected to newly created television values;

$V_I$—wages of the employees connected to creation of television values;

$m_I$—profit obtained out of the creation of television values.

2) Economic estimates of television services

$$C_2 + V_2 i + m_2 j + A_{STP} k = \text{television services}$$

, where

> $a_2$—expenses of past labor connected to creation of television services;
>
> $V_2i$—wages of employees connected to creation of television service;
>
> $m_2j$—;
>
> $A_{STP}k$—assimilated resource of spare time of population television services.

Since TV values and services have been recorded with the aid of complex numbers, operations with them should be performed according to the following rules of arithmetic:

a) addition of complex numbers;

$$z_1 + z_2 = (a_1 + b_1i) + (a_2 + b_2i) = (a_1 + a_2) + (b_1i + b_2i)$$

b) subtraction of complex numbers;

$$z_1 - z_2 = (a_1 + b_1i) - (a_2 + b_2i) = (a_1 - a_2) + (b_1i - b_2i)$$

c) multiplication of complex numbers;

$$z_1 z_2 = (a_1 + b_1i) \times (a_2 + b_2i) = a_1a_2 + a_1b_2i + a_2b_1i + b_1b_2i^2 = a_1a_2 + a_1b_2i +$$
$$+ a_2b_1i - b_1b_2 = (a_1a_2 - b_1b_2) + (a_1b_2 + a_2b_1)i$$

d) division of complex numbers.

$$\frac{z_1}{z_2} = \frac{a_1a_2 + b_1b_2}{a_2^2 + b_2^2} + \frac{(a_2b_1 - a_1b_2)i}{a_2^2 + b_2^2}$$

Using these arithmetic we can calculate the aggregate TV product.

## A. MOVEMENT OF TELEVISION VALUES AND SERVICES

Movement of these values and services in economic space can be represented as follows:

| | Process of production | Process of distribution | Process of exchange | Process of consumption |
|---|---|---|---|---|
| A. | Material TV product | Material TV product | Material TV product | Material TV product |
| B. | TV services | TV services | TV services | TV services |
| C. | Aggregate TV product | Aggregate TV product | Aggregate TV product | Aggregate TV product |

1. At every stage of movement of TV values and services there should be relevant estimates, criteria and indicators.

TV services are created, distributed and consumed at one time:

Time of creation of TV services
Time of distribution of TV services
Time of consumption of TV services
Time interval - T

### TABLE 1 THE SYSTEM OF ECONOMIC ESTIMATES

| | Estimates of production | Estimates of distribution | Estimates of exchange | Estimates of consumption |
|---|---|---|---|---|
| A. | Material TV product | Material TV product | Material TV product | Material TV product |
| B. | TV service with the account of $A_{STP}$ | TV service with the account of $A_{STP}$ | TV service with the account of $A_{STP}$ | TV service with the account of $A_{STP}$ |

| | | | |
|---|---|---|---|
| C. | Aggregate TV product with the account of $A_{STP}$ | Aggregate TV product with the account of $A_{STP}$ | Aggregate TV product with the account of $A_{STP}$ | Aggregate TV product with the account of $A_{STP}$ |

## TABLE 2 THE SYSTEM OF ECONOMIC ESTIMATES

| | Estimates of production | Estimates of distribution | Estimates of exchange | Estimates of consumption |
|---|---|---|---|---|
| A. | Material TV product | Material TV product | Material TV product | Material TV product |
| B. | TV service without taking into the account of $A_{STP}$ | TV service without taking into the account of $A_{STP}$ | TV service without taking into the account of $A_{STP}$ | TV service without taking into the account of $A_{STP}$ |
| C. | Aggregate TV product without taking into the account of $A_{STP}$ | Aggregate TV product without taking into the account of $A_{STP}$ | Aggregate TV product without taking into the account of $A_{STP}$ | Aggregate TV product without taking into the account of $A_{STP}$ |

If we subtract the first option of estimates of the movement of TV values, from the second option of estimates, we shall receive a system of errors:

Option 2 – Option 1 = $A_{STP}$

| | Errors in estimates of production | Errors in estimates of distribution | Errors in estimates of exchange | Errors in estimates of consumption |
|---|---|---|---|---|
| *A.* | $\Delta_{11}$ - errors | $\Delta_{12}$ - errors | $\Delta_{13}$ - errors | $\Delta_{14}$ - errors |
| *B.* | $\Delta_{21}$ - errors | $\Delta_{22}$ - errors | $\Delta_{23}$ - errors | $\Delta_{24}$ - errors |
| *C.* | $\Delta_{31}$ - errors | $\Delta_{32}$ - errors | $\Delta_{33}$ - errors | $\Delta_{34}$ - errors |

# 1. Values of the sixth power branch

| Branches | Volume of values of the sixth power branch (production use) | | | | Volume of values of the sixth power branch (non-production use) | | | | Aggregate volume of values of the sixth power branch | | | | | | |
|---|---|---|---|---|---|---|---|---|---|---|---|---|---|---|---|
| | № 1 | № 2 | № 3 | № 4 | № 5 | № 6 | № 7 | № 8 | № 9 | № 10 | № 11 | № 12 | Estimations | Criteria | Indicators |
| I branch — Production needs in values of the sixth power branch (estimation) $C_l + V_l^{P_i} i + m_l^{P_j} j$ | ▓ | | | | | | | | | | | | Estimations | Criteria | Indicators |
| | | ▓ | | | | | | | | | | | Estimations | Criteria | Indicators |
| | | | ▓ | | | | | | | | | | Estimations | Criteria | Indicators |
| | | | | ▓ | | | | | | | | | Estimations | Criteria | Indicators |
| II branch — Non-production needs in values of the sixth power branch (estimation) $V_l^{NP} i + m_l^{NP} j$ | | | | | ▓ | | | | | | | | Estimations | Criteria | Indicators |
| | | | | | | ▓ | | | | | | | Estimations | Criteria | Indicators |
| | | | | | | | ▓ | | | | | | Estimations | Criteria | Indicators |
| | | | | | | | | ▓ | | | | | Estimations | Criteria | Indicators |
| III branch — Complex production needs in values of the sixth power branch (estimation) | | | | | | | | | ▓ | | | | Estimations | Criteria | Indicators |
| | | | | | | | | | | ▓ | | | Estimations | Criteria | Indicators |
| | | | | | | | | | | | ▓ | | Estimations | Criteria | Indicators |
| | | | | | | | | | | | | ▓ | Estimations | Criteria | Indicators |
| | | | | | | | | | | | | | Estimations | Criteria | Indicators |

## 2. Services of the sixth power branch

| Branches | Volume of the sixth power branch services (production use) | | | | Volume of the sixth power branch services (non-production use) | | | | Aggregate volume of services of the sixth power branch | | | | | | |
|---|---|---|---|---|---|---|---|---|---|---|---|---|---|---|---|
| | № 1 | № 2 | № 3 | № 4 | № 5 | № 6 | № 7 | № 8 | № 9 | № 10 | № 11 | № 12 | Estimations | Criteria | Indicators |
| I branch | | | | | | | | | | | | | Estimations | Criteria | Indicators |
| Production needs in services of the sixth power branch (estimation) $C_2 + V_2^P i + m_2^P j$ | | | | | | | | | | | | | Estimations | Criteria | Indicators |
| | | | | | | | | | | | | | Estimations | Criteria | Indicators |
| | | | | | | | | | | | | | Estimations | Criteria | Indicators |
| II branch | | | | | | | | | | | | | Estimations | Criteria | Indicators |
| Non-production needs in services of the sixth power branch (estimation) $V_2^{NP} i + m_2^{NP} j + A_{rmd}$ | | | | | | | | | | | | | Estimations | Criteria | Indicators |
| | | | | | | | | | | | | | Estimations | Criteria | Indicators |
| | | | | | | | | | | | | | Estimations | Criteria | Indicators |
| III branch | | | | | | | | | | | | | Estimations | Criteria | Indicators |
| Complex needs in services of the sixth power branch (estimation) | | | | | | | | | | | | | Estimations | Criteria | Indicators |
| | | | | | | | | | | | | | Estimations | Criteria | Indicators |

I)  INDICATORS OF LONG-TERM PROVISION OF VALUES AND
    SERVICES OF THE SIXTH POWER BRANCH

A.  STRUCTURE OF LONG-TERM
    NEEDS OF VALUES OF THE SIXTH POWER BRANCH

**Thesis**      An increment ($\Delta$) of the volume of production needs in values of the sixth power branch

**Antithesis**  An increment ($\Delta$) of the volume of non-production needs in values of the sixth power branch

**Synthesis**   An increment ($\Delta$) of the volume of aggregate needs (both production and non-production character) in values of the sixth power branch

AA.  INDICATOR OF LONG-TERM
     «PROVISION OF THE SIXTH POWER BRANCH» (OF A
     PRODUCTION PURPOSE)

**Thesis**      Increment ($\Delta$) of the volume of values of sixth power branch production purpose ($\Delta$V-VAL-P)

**Antithesis**  Increment ($\Delta$) production needs in values of the sixth power branch

**Synthesis**   $$\frac{(\Delta\text{V-VAL-P})}{\text{Increment } (\Delta) \text{ production needs in values of the sixth power branch}} \text{ - indicator}$$

AAA.  INDICATOR OF LONG-TERM
      «PROVISION OF THE SIXTH POWER BRANCH» (OF A NON-
      PRODUCTION PURPOSE)

**Thesis**      Increment ($\Delta$) of the volume values of the sixth power branch non-production purpose ($\Delta$V-VAL-NP)

**Antithesis**  Increment ($\Delta$) non-production needs in values of the sixth power branch

**Synthesis**    $$\frac{(\Delta V\text{-VAL-NP})}{\text{Increment } (\Delta) \text{ non-production}}$$ - indicator

needs in values of the sixth power branch

| SYSTEM OF INDICATORS OF LONG-TERM OF THE SIXTH POWER BRANCH AS AGAINST FUNCTIONAL INDICATION | | | |
|---|---|---|---|
| | **THESIS** | **ANTITHESIS** | **SYNTHESIS** |
| **THESIS** Dialectical structure of long term aggregate values of the sixth power branch | An increment ($\Delta$) of the volume of values of the sixth power branch ($\Delta$VVP) for production purpose | An increment ($\Delta$) of the volume values of the sixth power branch non-production purpose ($\Delta$V-VAL-NP) | An increment ($\Delta$) of the volume of the aggregate values of the sixth power branch for production and non-production purpose |
| **ANTITHESIS** Dialectical structure of long-term needs of the sixth power branch | An increment ($\Delta$) of production needs in values of the sixth power branch ($\Delta$VVN) | An increment ($\Delta$) of non-production needs in values of the sixth power branch | An increment ($\Delta$) of aggregate needs in values of the sixth power branch of production and non-production purpose |
| **SYNTHESIS** Dialectical structure of indicator of long-term provision of the sixth power branch | An increment ($\Delta$) of the volume of values of the sixth power branch ($\Delta$VVP) for production purpose / An increment ($\Delta$) of production needs of values of the sixth power branch ($\Delta$VVN) | An increment ($\Delta$) of the volume values of the sixth power branch non-production purpose ($\Delta$VED-VAL-NP) / An increment ($\Delta$) of non-production needs in values of the sixth power branch | An increment ($\Delta$) of the aggregate values of the sixth power branch for production and non-production consumption / An increment ($\Delta$) of aggregate needs of the sixth power branch production and non-production purpose |

# PART 3

## THE UNESCO STOCK EXCHANGE INDEX

For many decades, the Dow Jones index has been protected from all directions; but today, right at the beginning of third millennium, we should re-examine the logic behind this index

Besides all those deficiencies, which are present in the «DJ» Index, today stock indices in the service sectors of the economy (intellectual, medical and Internet) are missing. This brings about a depressive state in stock brokers. We can not «feel» the services market.

Today the Dow Jones Index can be compared to the tip of an iceberg which one sees water.

That part which is underwater, in our case, is the services sector of the economy which remains a large riddle.

Today the «DJ» index should be arranged in logical reconstruction, a surgical, so to speak, operation.

Already today, at the first stage, the «DJ» index should be «cut out» into separate indices:

- Dow Jones Index 1—for the Material Sphere
- Dow Jones Index 2—for the Intellectual Sphere
- Dow Jones Index 3—for the Medical Sphere
- Dow Jones Index 4—for the Transport Sphere
- Dow Jones Index 5—for the Military Sphere
- Dow Jones Index 6—for the Internet Sphere
- Dow Jones Index 7—for the State Power Sphere

Only in such a, so to speak, autonomous version, the set of the Dow Jones Index will increase the adequacy of the reflection of the relations of stock exchange.

I suggest refusing the old logic of constructing the exchange index. In new indices, I use other the logic.

I suggest following exchange indices of autonomous spheres:

The Government Sphere—Stock Exchange Indices

The Material Sphere—Stock Exchange Indices

The Mass Media—Stock Exchange Indices

The Intellectual Sphere—Stock Exchange Indices

The Internet Sphere—Stock Exchange Indices

The Medical Sphere—Stock Exchange Indices

The Transportation Sphere—Stock Exchange Indices

The Military Sphere—Stock Exchange Indices

These autonomous exchange indices will allow us to place everything where it belongs, to leave, so to speak, the «Triple cocktail» (industry, transport and HAS), and to proceed to «clean» exchange indices (without the supplements). In this suggested alternative, we shall not have a headache because of the poor quality side of the indices.

## Synopsis

In USA, Euro countries, the intellectual sphere represents a huge economical system. With each passing year, it expands its boundaries, pushing out other economical spheres.

1. The financial institutions market poorly imagine what is going in the intellectual segment of the market.

The inquisitive reader may ask the question: Why are the stock exchange indices of intellectual sphere necessary?

Why do we overlook the fact that in the total expenses of the economy considerable proportion includes the expenses of the Intellectual and Internet spheres? The nation; monetary unit depends on the state of the economy of the intellectual sphere of a country, whether there will be «strong» or «soft» currency.

We should have at our disposal quality information about the state of the economy of the Intellectual Sphere, just as we would of a separate country or as a separate continent (Europe, North America, South America, Asia, Africa). This is the essence of the «business monitoring» of the Intellectual Sphere.

I suggesting arranging on axes X, Y, Z, noted above the vectors aa, bb, CC,

aa1—The Educational Sphere—Stock Exchange Index

bb1—The Enlightenment Sphere—Stock Exchange Index

CC1—The Entertainment Sphere—Stock Exchange Index

Using a three-dimensional reference system. The total exchange index for the Intellectual Sphere can be introduced as follows:

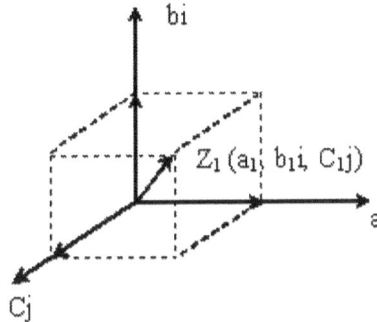

These three indices characterize only the exchange relations.

$$Z = aa1 + bb1i + CC1j$$

At creating the total system of indices, we should remember other economical relations, where the resources of Intellectual Sphere are involved, on each of economical relations, there should be unique, special indices:

- Index of production

- Index of distribution

- Index of consumption

- Index of exchange

## A. EDUCATION STOCK EXCHANGE INDEX

An analysis of the economic literature on the problems of the educational sphere show that many categories and conceptions used have become obsolete. They do not correspond to present day demands.

Today the stream of school children is considered a statistical component and for this reason it is not included in the cost of educational services. This way of assessment of educational services, to my mind, looks distorted, since:

- part of the resources is considered as economic;
- part of the resources is considered as statistical.

This is one of the existing paradoxes in the economic theory of the educational sphere. In the economic theory of the educational sphere there is a significant number of unsolved problems.

Researchers of economic problems of education often refer to the necessity of applying new methods, criteria and indicators. However, the essence of the new approaches is not specified.

Such a situation cannot go on for years.

I suggest to use unconventional approaches and methods, and more essentially, to apply complex numbers.

## THE MACROECONOMY OF THE EDUCATIONAL SPHERE WITH COMPLEX NUMBERS—QUATERNIONS

Format: Paperback
Size: 6 x 9
Pages: 230
ISBN: 9963-633-42-0
Published: Cyprus, August 2003

ISBN - 13: 978-0-595-41776-6 pbk

Published USA 2006

## B. ENTERTAINMENT STOCK EXCHANGE INDEX

The inhabitants of the ancient Rome demanded bread and entertainment from their emperor. And there were required more and more «shows».

Elephants, lions, tigers and home animals were brought from all over the Empire to arrange shows. The shows used to continue for 300 days a year. The shows continued during daytime, in the evenings and all nights long. Now it is very difficult to imagine the huge amount of the people enlisted to arrange the shows. They are thousands, hundred thousands; one of them used to catch the animals, others delivered the animals by sea and by land, and others used to prepare the animals for the shows. This was taking place for hundred years.

Now it is difficult to find out a proportion of the expenses in the budget of the Rome Empire to arrange the shows.

What was a proportion of the Gross Domestic Product at the periods of 50, 20 and 10 years before the Empire collapsed?

Is it possible that an augmentation of the expenses for a show sector was one of the main reasons the Empire collapsed?

We are not in the position to answer the questions, and a topicality of the «bread» and «show» theme still remains. The people got used to the shows. This is the second constituent of our every day life. Today we are facing 2000, a new millennium, and the economic theory does not have any provisions so far, which make it possible to set up an amount of the «shows» required for a state with small, average and large population. How much «bread» and how many «shows» will there be in a «consumer's basket» in 5 years, in 10 years? The question is possible to be replied as regards «the bread» only, and you will not find any answer for «the shows» due to the lack of an economic theory for a show sector. It is not developed yet.

- As regards the «show» market, the only thing we know is that it exists;
- We do not know its absolute borders;
- We do not know an inner structure of the market;
- We do not know how it influences the other markets;
- We do not know the critical points in the «show sector» development.

**Today the «DJ» Index does not work in the «field» of entertainment services**

Maybe the time has come to create the indices of the entertainment sphere.

For example, «Catherine-Zeta Jones index» (for the cinema distribution) or «Yellow Submarine Index» for the show sphere. And why not?

## C. CINEMA STOCK EXCHANGE INDEX

The year 1995 turned out to be as successful as 1994 for the Buena Vista company. Not only did it top the list of income in the USA film market, but it also earned over a billion dollars from distributing film in the USA and Canada. Warner Brothers, as last year, was in honorable second place, while Sony spurted through the last weeks of 1995 and thus managed to take third place. Buena Vista, Walt Disney's film distributor, received an income of one billion, ten million dollars, almost as much as its income in 1994. It should be noted that before 1994 no US Company ever exceeded the billion-dollar barrier income. In total the American film companies made a profit in the region of 5 billion and 510 million dollars in 1995. A rise in ticket prices meant that they sold in smaller quantities than in the previous year. In 1995, a total of 1.28 billion tickets were sold. That was two per cent less than the total of sales of 1994, when 1.29 billion tickets were sold. The sum total of film distribution in 1994 was 5.4 billion dollars. Only seven films in 1995 exceeded the income barrier of a hundred million, taking into account the sum total of film distribution in the USA and Canada. The greatest hit of last year was Warner Brothers' «Batman Forever», which collected nearly 184 million dollars. Ten films exceeded an income barrier equal to 100 million dollars in 1994, including two, which collected 300 million dollars each. These were «Paramount»'s «Forrest Gump» and «Buena Vista»'s «The lion King». These films took third and fifth place respectively in the level of received incomes in the entire history of the US film market. The 1994 hit «Batman Forever» was followed by the 1995 hits «Apollo 13» (Universal, $172.1 million), «Toy Story» (Buena Vista, $150 million), «Pochahontas» (Buena Vista, $141.5 million), «Ace Ventura: When Nature Calls» (Warner Brothers, $105 million), «Casper» (Universal, $100.3 million), «Die Hard With Avengeance» (20th Century Fox, $ 100.1 million). All figures are based on the total income from film distribution in the USA and Canada reached on January 1, 1996.

The top ten of 1995 collected a total of 1.23 billion, $ 352 million (22 per cent) less than the total of income of the top ten films of 1994. The top 25 distribution hits of 1995 made a total of $ 2.28 billion some $ 322 (12 per cent) less then the comparable total for 1994 that amounted to $ 2.61 billion. Expert opinion maintained that the films of 1995 were less entertaining. That is why only seven of them exceeded 100 million in income. Besides, it is well known that income from films grow and contract in cycles, each cycle lasting approximately 3-4 years. Revenue of 1.15 billion tickets sold was 1991 income growth from film distribution in the US and Canada, at least in the near future, is predicted to be held up. According to long-standing observations, such stagnation usually lasts from a year, to a year-and-a-half.

The economic theory of the intellectual sphere prompts that there is a paradox in the «logic»: economic processes disregard time as a factor. It is confirmed by the parameters used in the intellectual sphere: «visit», «cinema goers» etc. From this context the following questions arise:

1) How is it possible to investigate the economic processes in the intellectual sphere without considering the duration of visits to the establishments of Enlightenment, Education and Entertainment institutions, etc?

2) What effect do visitors, as a resource, to theatres, museums, churches, cinemas, schools, universities have on economic indicators?

I propose to consider the economic processes of the intellectual sphere, which include temporary components. The flow of visitors to museums, libraries, shows enterprises, schools and universities is a resource involved in the process of creating intellectual services. In relation to this, the population's spare time is also a resource component of intellectual services. We have no reasons to exclude this flow of resources from the calculations of basic economic indicators. If we display reluctance in using these resources in the calculations, the economic processes may become distorted.

The noted above problems are reviewed in the book:

**Economics: Enlightenment and Entertainment**

**Synopsis**

In Economics: Enlightenment and Entertainment, the author suggests that we give necessary consideration to the following problems:

- a new structure of enlightenment and entertainment services;

- a horizontal structure of the enlightenment and entertainment market.

Format: Paperback
Size: 6 x 9
Pages: 280
ISBN: 0-595-19166-5
Published: September 2001

## THE MACROECONOMY OF THE INTERNET SPHERE WITH COMPLEX NUMBERS

Introduction

In the economy of the Internet sphere there is quite number of problems that need to be solved. Judge for yourselves:

- until recently, the Internet sphere has never been examined as an economic system;

- peculiarities of the Internet components haven't been worked out;

- peculiarities of the economic relations in the Internet sphere haven't been defined;

- essence of the categories—Internet values, Internet services, complex Internet product—hasn't been established;

- economic estimations of the Internet values are defined separately from the economic estimations of the Internet services;

- «On Line Time» (OLT) is not considered as an economic resource;

- the OLT resource is not included in the cost of the Internet services;

- specific features of the economic estimations are connected with the movement of the Internet values and Internet services.

The economic criteria of the effectiveness of the use of resources in the framework of production, distribution, exchange and consumption have not been explained.

The outlines of these problems become clearer and significantly better understood if Internet values, Internet services and the OLT are examined in a three-dimensional space.

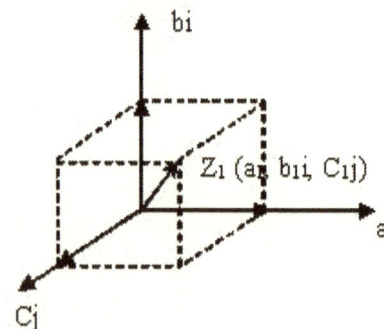

where

(a) is the cost estimation of Internet values (computers, programmes etc.)

(bi) represents the expenses connected with the creation of Internet services (OLT not included)

(Cj) is the cost estimation of the assimilated OLT resource.

The total vector z is formulated as follows: $Z = a + bi + Cj$

The z vector assumes different values depending on the three components a, b and c.

If the particular OLT resource is not taken into account, the Z vector is being examined in a two-dimensional space, without the Cj component.

If we look at the reproduction of the Internet sphere from this position, i.e. without the «On Line Time» (OLT) resource, it will mean that one of the basic Internet incoming resources is excluded. As a result, the economic estimations are decreased by the amount of not included OLT resource.

## THE MACROECONOMY OF INTERNET SPHERE WITH COMPLEX NUMBERS

ISBN 0-595-26322-4

Page: 228

# PART 4

## REPRODUCTION OF THE INTELLECTUAL SPHERE

A. THE RESOURCE STREAMS IN THE INTELLECTUAL SPHERE OF PRODUCTION

B. THE REPRODUCTION OF THE INTELLECTUAL SPHERE IN TERMS OF ASSIMILATED AND PAID RESOURCE OF POPULATION SPARE TIME

C. THE REPRODUCTION OF THE INTELLECTUAL SPHERE IN TERMS OF ASSIMILATED AND PARTIALLY PAID RESOURCE OF POPULATION SPARE TIME

D. INTER BRANCH BALANCE OF INTELLECTUAL PRODUCTION

## A. THE RESOURCE STREAMS IN THE INTELLECTUAL SPHERE OF PRODUCTION

The author of the present book considers an intellectual sphere as an economic system that consists of three Divisions:

| Intellectual Production | 1st Division of intellectual production | Book publishing Newspaper-magazine production Film production | Intellectual values (books, journals, pictures) |
| --- | --- | --- | --- |
| | 2nd Division of intellectual production | Enlightenment, (Culture, Art, Church) Education (schools, colleges, universities) | Intellectual services of education |
| | 3rd Division of intellectual production | Entertainment branch (Sport-entertaining, Film distribution, Radio, TV) | Entertainment services |

There is an interaction of resources taking place between the branches of Divisions 1, 2 & 3—books, pictures, films enter libraries, schools, colleges, museums, «Film distribution», «TV Broadcasting», «Radio Broadcasting» wherein the intellectual services are created.

The financial resources of the intellectual production are directed:

1.  to purchase equipment and special instruments of labor required to produce the intellectual values and services;

2.  to employ workers (labor resources) to produce the intellectual values and services.

*Scheme № 1*

---

### DIALECTICAL SCHEME
### OF RESOURCE MOTION IN THE INTELLECTUAL SPHERE OF PRODUCTION

**Thesis**      An aggregate of resources coming into intellectual production Division I

**Antithesis**  An aggregate of resources coming into intellectual production Division II:      a) enlightenment, education branches;

Division III:           b) entertainment branches.

**Synthesis**   A whole resource stream coming into the intellectual sphere of production.

---

As a result of an economic linkage of these resource streams the working time of all those working in the intellectual sphere of production is assimilated, on one hand, and, on the other, the population's spare time assimilated within «Enlightenment», «Education» and «Entertainment» branches.

In general, a scheme of the resource motion in the intellectual sphere looks as follows:

$\Delta C_{IM} = \Delta C_{1I}^{IM} + \Delta C_{2I}^{IM} + \Delta C_{3I}^{IM}$ —resource stream out of material production

A, B, C—assimilated resource STP of the employers in the intellectual sphere by the «enlightenment», «education» system branches;

D, E, L—a resource STP of the intellectual sphere employers assimilated by the show branches.[15]

Besides, the resource STP of the relatively autonomous spheres is assimilated: $STP_1 STP_2 STP_3 STP_4$

$STP_5 + STP_6 + STP_7$—spare time resource of the intellectual sphere employers.

The resources thathave entered the intellectual sphere alter as a result of special technologies utilization, thus forming up the outcoming streams. The streams are written down as follows:

*Scheme № 2*

---

### DIALECTICAL SCHEME
### OF A RESOURCE MOTION OUT OF THE INTELLECTUAL
### SPHERE OF PRODUCTION

**Thesis** A stream of intellectual values—books, newspapers, magazines, films, church utensils, TV- and Radio-equipment, etc., created in the branches of intellectual production Division I (I)

**Antithesis** A stream of intellectual services—of «enlightenment», «education» (E) and «entertainment services» (S) created in the service sector of the intellectual sphere.

**Synthesis** A whole stream of intellectual values and services created in the intellectual sphere of production (I + E + S).

---

Three main streams coming out of the intellectual sphere form up three groups of the branches:

1st Group—the branches producing material-intellectual values: books, newspapers, magazines, films, TV and Radio equipment—(I);

2nd Group—sub-branches of the «enlightenment», «education» system—(E);

3rd Group—show-branches—(S).

I propose these three groups to be combined into a unique economic system that is taken down as follows:

---

15 $A^{III}_{STP} = A^{S}_{STP}$

$$\begin{cases} C_1 + V_1 + m_1 \quad = I_1 \cap STP_H \\ C_2 + V_2 + A^E_{STP} = I_2 \cap STP_H \\ C_3 + V_3 + A^S_{STP} = I_3 \cap STP_H \end{cases}$$

, whereat

$C_1, C_2, C_3$—the past labor expended while creating the intellectual values and services $D_1, D_2, D_3$;

$V_1, V_2, V_3$—wages (a direct labor) of the employers of IP Divisions I, II & III;

$A^E_{STP}, A^S_{STP}$—resource STP assimilated by «enlightenment», «education» and «entertainment» branches and completely paid.

As per the scheme above a Gross Domestic Product (GDP) of the intellectual sphere of production would look as follows:

$$(C_1 + C_2 + C_3) + (V_1 + V_2 + V_3) + m_1 + (A^E_{STP} + A^S_{STP}) = D_1 + D_2 + D_3 = GDP$$

Net Domestic Product (NDP) created within the frames of an intellectual sphere is taken down as follows:

$$(V_1 + V_2 + V_3) + m_1 + (A^E_{STP} + A^S_{STP}) = NDP$$

Net Income (NI) created within the intellectual sphere looks as follows:

$$m_1 + (A^E_{STP} + A^S_{STP}) = NI$$

The values newly created in intellectual sphere Division $I_{ID}$ break up into four streams: $\Delta_1$—is directed to restore a material and technical basis of intellectual production Division I, $\Delta_2$, $\Delta_3$ are directed to develop means of labor of IP Divisions II & III.[16*] Another portion of the product of labor of Division I is directed to meet needs of people in the material-intellectual values $\Delta_4$.

_____

16    An accumulation of the production means of IP Divisions I, II & III takes place to a considerable extent on the account of the activity result of Division I of the material production, a building construction $\Delta C^{CIM}_{11}$, $\Delta C^{CIM}_{21}$ and $\Delta C^{CIM}_{31}$ in particular.

The same schematically looks as follows:

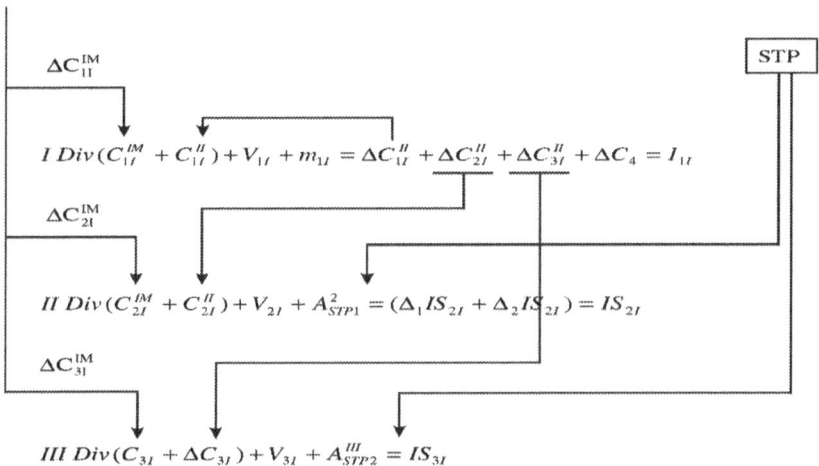

An expanded reproduction of the intellectual sphere is carried out in the case of additional investments, when in Division I of the intellectual sphere there were created more means and instruments of labor than it was required in the previous cycle. In this case a reproduction process becomes an expanded one.

There are a lot of schemes of the intellectual sphere reproduction. Thus, for instance, an alteration of the ratio value a, b, g in a system of equations may result in obtaining a considerable number of modifications of the intellectual production schemes.

The reproduction schemes of an intellectual process:

$$\begin{cases} \alpha_1 C_1 + \beta_1 V_1 + \gamma_1 m_1 = I_1 \\ \alpha_2 C_2 + \beta_2 V_2 + \gamma_2 m_2 + A_{STP}^E = I_2 \\ \alpha_3 C_3 + \beta_3 V_3 + \gamma_3 m_3 + A_{STP}^{III} = I_3 \end{cases} *$$

Modification I

$$\alpha_1 > \alpha_2, \beta_1 > \beta_2, \gamma_1 > \gamma_2,$$
$$\alpha_2 > \alpha_3, \beta_2 > \beta_3, \gamma_2 > \gamma_3.$$

$$\alpha_1 > \alpha_2, \beta_1 > \beta_2, \gamma_1 > \gamma_2,$$

Modification II    $\alpha_2 = \alpha_3, \beta_2 = \beta_3, \gamma_2 = \gamma_3.$ and other modifications. [17]

, whereat

$\alpha, \beta, \gamma$ - ratios.

The intellectual production schemes are classified using «equality» and «inequality» between past labor expenses, direct labor expenses, aggregate labor expenses, that create the intellectual values and services.

The reproduction schemes of the intellectual sphere in terms of 100 per cent payment for the resource STP assimilated by «enlightenment», «education» and «enlightenment» branches are considered here. In my opinion, this variant rarely takes place. The intellectual sphere of reproduction mostly takes place in terms of a partial payment for the assimilated resource STP, i.e. a portion of the assimilated resource is paid for and another portion is not.

## 2.  THE REPRODUCTION OF THE INTELLECTUAL SPHERE IN TERMS OF ASSIMILATED AND PAID RESOURCE STP

A reproduction of the intellectual sphere when the assimilated resource STP is paid. In this variant it comes out as an income in Division II and in Division III $m_3 = A_{STP}^S.$

---

[17] $A_{STP}^{III} = A_{STP}^S$

A peculiar feature of the considered scheme 1 of the intellectual sphere reproduction is as follows:

**_First_**  past labor expenses in intellectual production Divisions I, II & III are equal and come to 2000 C;

**_Second_** direct labor expenses in intellectual production Division I, II & III come to 1000 V each;

**_Third_**  the «enlightenment», «education» and «entertainment» branches assimilate an equal amount of STP that comes to 4000 stp;

**_Fourth_** a sum of the intellectual services of intellectual production Divisions II & III ($D_2 + D_3$) comes to 14000 c.u., and the same exceeds the intellectual values of Division I about five times;

**_Fifth_**  a peculiarity of the intellectual production GDP created as per scheme is that:

- past (aggregate) labor expenses $C_1 + C_2 + C_3 = 6000$ come to 33 per cent of GDP;

- direct labor expenses $V_1 + V_2 + V_3 = 3000$. This comes to 16 per cent of GDP;

- common expenses on creation of the intellectual production GDP come to 9000 c.u.

- a volume of the assimilated resource STP comes to 44 per cent of GDP—a Gross Domestic Product of the intellectual production.

As in scheme № 9.1, a volume of the material-intellectual values created by the branches of intellectual production Division I $\underbrace{I(C + V + m)}_{4000}$ is less than past labor expenses while creating the values of Division I and intellectual services bf Divisions II & III.

$$\underbrace{I(C + V + m)}_{4000} \; < \; \underbrace{IC + IIC + IIIC}_{6000}$$

$$2000\ C_1 + 1000\ V_1 + 1000\ m_1 = 4000\ c.u.$$

$$2000\ C_2 + 1000\ V_2 + 0.4 \cdot 10000\ hour = 7000\ c.u.$$

$$2000\ C_3 + 1000\ V_3 + 0.4 \cdot 10000\ hour = 7000\ c.u.$$

$$6000\ C + 3000\ V + 1000\ m_1 + 8000_{STP} = 18\ 000\ c.u.$$

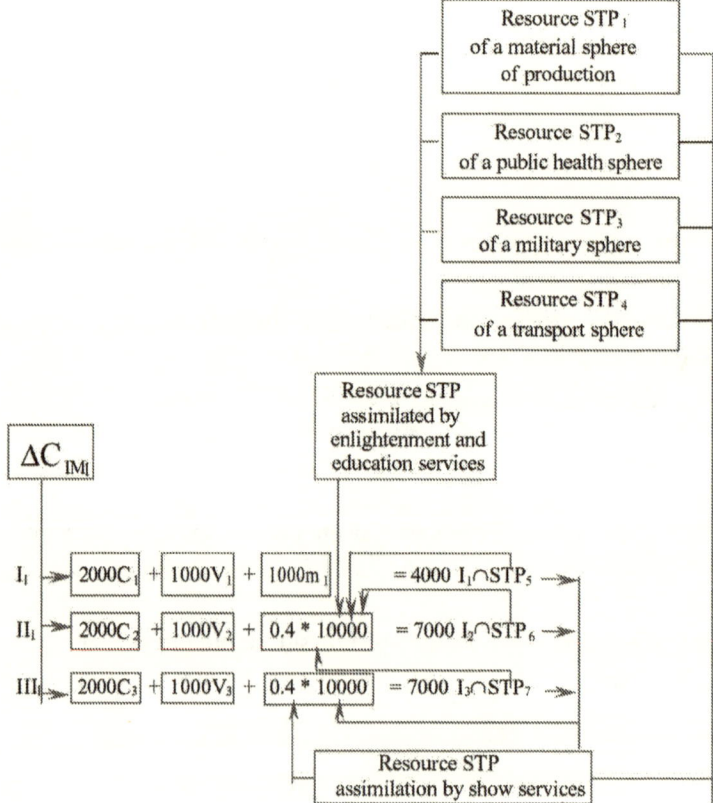

$$6000C + 3000V + 1000m_1 + 8000_{STP} = 18000\ I \cap STP^{18}$$

18    $\Delta C_{IM}$—a resource stream out of material sphere (buildings, communications) $STP_1$, $STP_2$, $STP_3$, $STP_4$, - a spare time of the employers of the material sphere, public health, military and transport spheres respectively

| Divisions | Indicators of Scheme № 1 | | | | | | %  | |
|---|---|---|---|---|---|---|---|---|
| | Inner correlations | | | | | | | |
| I | $C_1$ | | | | | | | $NI_1$ |
| | | $V_1$ | | | $C/V = 2$ | | | | |
| | | | $m_1$ | | $V/m = 1$ | | | | |
| | | $C_1 + V_1 + m_1$ | | | $m/V = 1$ | | | 4000 | $I_1$ |
| | | | | | $m/(C+V) = 0.33$ | | | | |
| | | | | | $m/(V+m) = 0.5$ | | | | |
| | | | | | $(V_1+m_1)/C_1 = 0.5$ | | | | |
| II | Expenses of production of services of education | | | $C_2$ | | | | | $NI_2$ |
| | | | | $V_2$ | | $C/V = 2$ | | | |
| | Net income | | | | $A^E_{STP}$ | $V/(_{STP}) = 0.25$ | | | |
| | | | | | | $(m + A_{STP})/V = 4$ | | | |
| | | | $C_1 + V_1 + m_1 + A^E_{STP}$ | | | | | 7000 | $I_2$ |
| | | | | | | $4000/3000 = 4/3$ | | | |
| | | | | | | $E_{STP}/(C+V) = 4/3$ | | | |
| | | | | | | $(V_2 + E_{STP})/I_2 = 5/7$ | | | |
| III | | | Production expenses of show services | | $C_3$ | | | | $NI_3$ |
| | | | | | | $V_3$ | $C/V=2$ | | |
| | | | Net income | | | | $A^{III}_{STP}$  1/4 | | |
| | | | | | $C_3 + V_3 + A^E_{STP} =$ | | | 7000 | $I_3$ |
| | | | | | $(m + A^E_{STP})/(C_3+V_3)= 4/3$ | | | | $I_1/I_2 = 4/7$ |
| | | | | | | | | | $I_2/I_3 = 1$ |
| | | | | | $(V_3 + A_{STP})/I_3 = 5/7$ | | | | $(I_2+I_3)/ЦИ_1$ $= 14/3$ |
| $I_1$ | $C_1 + V_1 + m_1$ | | | | | | | | |
| $I_2$ | | | | $C_2 + V_2 + A^E_{STP}$ | | | | | |
| $I_3$ | | | | | $C_3 + V_3 + A^E_{STP}$ | | | | |
| $I_{TOTAL}$ | $6000C + 3000V + 1000m + 8000_{STP}$ | | | | | | | 18000 | |

Should we assert that the cost of the capital assets is considerably higher in IP Division I than that of IP Divisions II & III, one of the variants of the structure for the intellectual production would be as follows.

$$4000\ C_1 + 1000\ V_1 + 1000\ m_1 \qquad = 6000\ c.u.$$

$$2000\ C_2 + 1000\ V_2 + 0.4 \cdot 10000\ hour = 7000\ c.u.$$

$$2000\ C_3 + 1000\ V_3 + 0.4 \cdot 10000\ hour = 7000\ c.u.$$

$$8000\ C + 3000\ V + 1000\ m_1 + 8000\ stp = 20\ 000\ c.u.$$

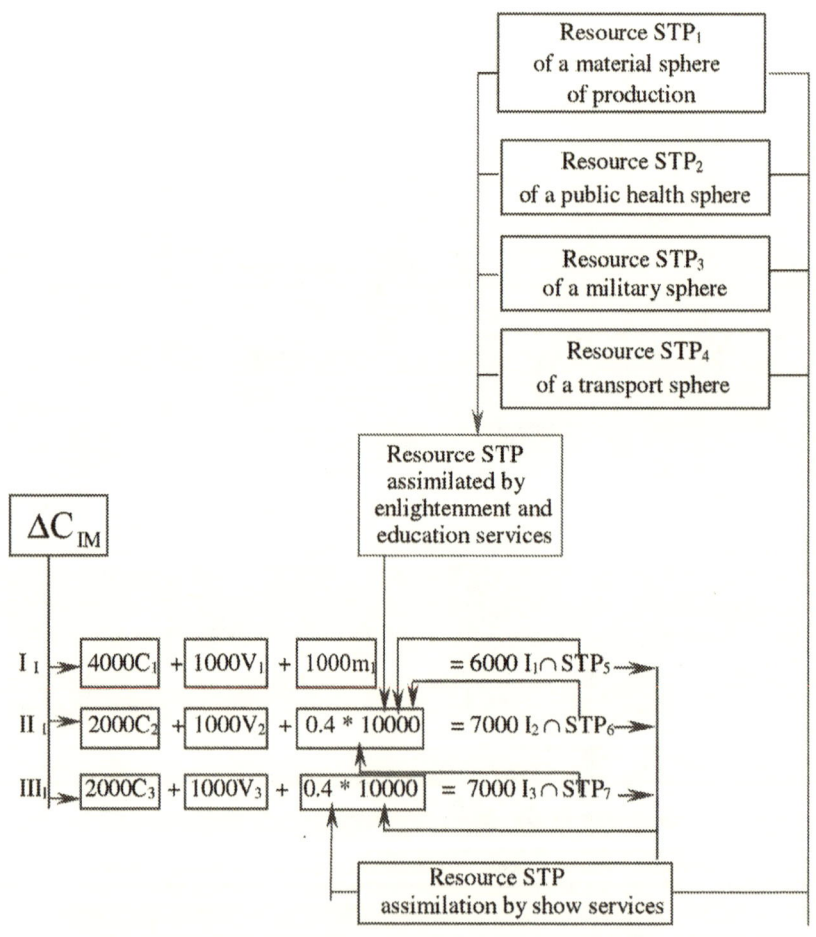

$$8000C + 3000V + 1000m_1 + 8000_{STP} = 20000\ I \cap STP$$

| Divisions | Indicators of Scheme № 2 | | % | |
|---|---|---|---|---|
| | **Inner correlations** | | | |
| I | $C_1$ | | | NI₁ |
| | $V_1$ — $C/V = 4$ | | | |
| | $m_1$ — $V/m = 1$ | | | |
| | $C_1+V_1+m_1$ — $m/V = 1$ | | 6000 | I₁ |
| | $m_1/(C_1+V_1) = 1$ | | | |
| | $m_1/(V_1+m_1) = 0.5$ | | | |
| | $(V_1+m_1)/C_1 = 0.33$ | | | |
| II | Expenses of production of services of education — $C_2$ | | | NI₂ |
| | $V_2$ — $C/V = 2$ | | | |
| | $m_2$ — $V/(m+A_{STP}) = 1/4$ | | | |
| | Net income — $A^E_{STP}$ — $(m + A_{STP})/V = 4$ | | | |
| | $C_1+V_1+A^E_{STP}$ | | 7000 | I₂ |
| | $A^E_{STP}/(C+V) = 4/3$ | | | |
| | $(V_2 + E_{STP})/I_2 = 5/7$ | | | |
| III | Production expenses of show services — $C_3$ | | | NI₃ |
| | $V_3$ | | | |
| | Net income — $A^{III}_{STP}$  1 1/4 | | | |
| | $C_3+V_3+A^E_{STP}$ | | 7000 | I₃ |
| | $A^E_{STP}/(C_3+V_3) = 4/5$ | | | $I_1/I_2 = 6/7$ |
| | | | | $I_2/I_3 = 1$ |
| | $(V_3+A_{STP})/I_3 = 5/7$ | | | $(I_2+I_3)/ЦI_1 = 2.33$ |
| I₁ | $C_1+V_1+m_1$ | | | |
| I₂ | $C_2+V_2+A^E_{STP}$ | | | |
| I₃ | $C_3+V_3+A^E_{STP}$ | | | |
| I_TOTAL | $8000C+3000V+1000m+8000_{STP}$ | | 20000 | |

A peculiarity of the considered scheme (№2) of the intellectual sphere reproduction is as follows:

*First*    past labor expenses in IP Division I are considerably higher than those in IP Divisions II & III:

$$C_1 = 2 C_2,\ C_1 = 2 C_3,\text{ at the same time } C_1 = C_2 + C_3 = 4000 \text{ c.u.;}$$

*Second* direct labor expenses (as wages) on assimilation of the spare time resource within «enlightenment», «education» branches and show branches are equal; $V_1 = V_2 = V_3 = 1000$ c.u.;

*Third* the branches of Divisions I, II & III assimilate resource STP at the volume of 4000 conv. hours each;

*Fourth* cost evaluation of the labor results of IP Divisions II & III $(D_2 + D_3)$ exceeds the cost of the product of labor of Division I - $D_1$ by 2.33 times;

*Fifth* a peculiar feature of the intellectual production GDP created as per scheme is:

- past labor expenses $(C_1 + C_2 + C_3) = 8000$ come to 40 per cent in the whole volume of IP GDP;

- direct labor expenses $(V_1 + V_2 + V_3) = 3000$ come to 15 per cent in the whole volume of IP GDP;

- expenses on creating the intellectual production GDP come to 55 per cent;

- a volume of the assimilated resource STP comes to 40 per cent of GDP.

As regards Scheme C 2, the volume of the material-intellectual values created by the branches of Division I $(C + V + m) = 6000$ c.u. is less than the past labor expenses spent to create the values of Division I and the intellectual services of IP Divisions II & III.

$$I(C + V + m) < IC + IIC + IIIC$$

$$\underbrace{\qquad}_{6000} \qquad \underbrace{\qquad}_{8000}$$

In other words, as against the scheme there is no reproduction of the intellectual sphere taking place as there is <u>no restoration</u> of past labor expenses spent to create $D_1, D_2, D_3$. 2000 c.u. is missing.

The above structure gives a supposition that the production structure of the intellectual services of «enlightenment», «education» is identical to the production structure of the show services. And there may be several variants in reality.

Variant I—the factors participating in the production of the intellectual services of «enlightenment», «education» exceed factors in «entertainment» branches by two to four times.

**_Scheme № 3_**

$6000\,C_1 + 3000\;V_1 + 2000\;m_1 \qquad = 11000$ c.u.

$3000\,C_2 + 1500\;V_2 + 0.4 \cdot 15000$ hr $= 10500$ c.u.

$2000\,C_3 + 1000\;V_3 + 0.4 \cdot 10000$ hr $= 7000$ c.u.

$11000\,C + 5500\,V + 2000\;m_1 + 10000$ stp $= 28\,500$ c.u.

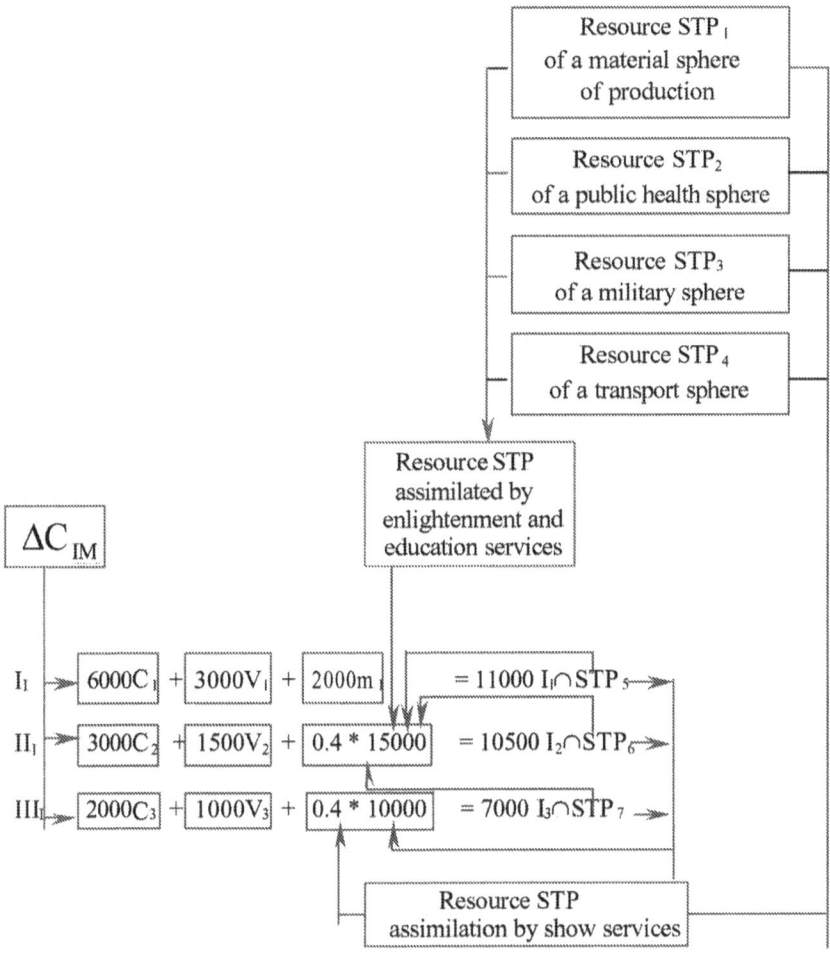

$11000C + 5500V + 2000m_1 + 10000\,{}_{STP} = 28500\; I \cap STP$

| Divisions | Indicators of Scheme № 3 | | | | | |
|---|---|---|---|---|---|---|
| | Inner correlations | | | | | % |
| I | $C_1$ 6000 | | | | | |
| | | $V_1$ 3000 | $C/V = 2$ | | | NI₁ |
| | | | $m_1$ | $V/m = 1.5$ | | |
| | $C_1 + V_1 + m_1$ | | $m/V = 2/3$ | | 11000 | $I_1$ |
| | | | $m/(C+V) = 0.22$ | | | |
| | | | $m/(V+m) = 0.4$ | | | |
| | | | $(V_1+m_1)/C_1 = 0.45$ | | | |
| II | Expenses of production of services of education | $C_2$ | | | | |
| | | $V_2$ | | $C/V = 2$ | | NI₂ |
| | Net income | $A^E_{STP}$ - | | $V/A_{STP} = 0.25$ | | |
| | | | | $A_{STP}/V = 4$ | | |
| | $C_1 + V_1 + A^E_{STP}$ | | | | 10500 | $I_2$ |
| | | | | $A_{STP}/(C+V) = 1.33$ | | |
| | | | | $(V_2 + E_{STP})/I_2 = 0.71$ | | |
| III | Production expenses of show services | $C_3$ | | | | |
| | | $V_3$ | | | | NI₃ |
| | Net income | $A^{III}_{STP}$ | | | | |
| | | | | | 4000 | |
| | $C_3 + V_3 + A^E_{STP}$ | | | | 7000 | $I_3$ |
| | | | | | | $I_1/I_2 = 1.04$ |
| | | | $A^{III}_{STP}/(C_3+V_3) = 4/3$ | | | $I_2/I_3 = 1.5$ |
| | | | $(V_3 + A_{STP})/I_3 = 5/7$ | | | $(I_2+I_3)/I_1 = 1.59$ |
| $I_1$ | $C_1 + V_1 + m_1$ | | | | | |
| $I_2$ | $C_2 + V_2 + A^E_{STP}$ | | | | | |
| $I_3$ | $C_3 + V_3 + A^E_{STP}$ | | | | | |
| $I_{TOTAL}$ | 11000C + 5500V + 1000m + 10000$_{STP}$ | | | | 28500 | |

A peculiarity of considered Scheme № 3 of the intellectual sphere reproduction is that:

**_First_**  past labor expenses ($C_1$) in intellectual sphere Division I are 2 times higher than the analogous expenses in Division II and three times higher than those of IP Division III;

*Second* direct labor expenses as against the scheme are 2 times less in Division II than those of Division I, and the same of Division III is 3 times less than of Division I;

*Third* an assimilation of the resource STP in Division II comes to 6000 conv. hours, and in the show branches—4000 conv. hours.;

*Fourth* a sum of the intellectual services $(D_2 + D_3)$ of IP Divisions II & III comes to $(10500 + 7000) = 17500$ c.u., 61,4 per cent of IP GDP;

*Fifth* a characteristic feature of the IP GDP created as against the scheme is as follows:

- the past labor expenses in the intellectual sphere $(C_1 + C_2 + C_3)$ come to 11000 or 38,6 per cent in the whole volume of IP GDP;

- the direct labor expenses $(V_1 + V_2 + V_3)$ come to 5500 c.u. or 19,3 per cent in the whole volume of IP GDP;

- the common expenses on creation of IP GDP come to 11000 c.u. +5500 c.u. = 16500 c.u.;

- a volume of the assimilated resource STP comes to 57,9 per cent of IP GDP;

*Sixth* as regards Scheme C3 of the intellectual sphere reproduction, a volume of the values created in IP Division I (11000 c.u.) is equal to the past labor expenses that have taken place while creating the values of Division I and the intellectual services of IP Divisions II & III.

$$I(C + V + m) \;=\; \underbrace{IC + IIC + IIIC}$$

$$\underbrace{\phantom{I(C + V + m)}}_{11000} \qquad \underbrace{\phantom{IC + IIC + IIIC}}_{11000}$$

In other words, the intellectual values created in IP Division I completely compensate the past labor expenses in Divisions I, II & III of the intellectual sphere;

*Seventh* a summary volume of the intellectual services created in the branches of «enlightenment», «education» and in «entertainment» branches, i.e. $D_2 + D_3 = 17500$ c.u., that exceeds a volume of the intellectual values produced in IP Division I:

**17500 - 11000 = 6500 c.u.**

The excess reflects the fact of the advantageous development of the branches that produce intellectual services over production of the intellectual values.

$8000C_1 + 4000 V_1 + 6000 m_1$     $= 18000$ c.u.

$8000C_2 + 4000 V_2 + 0.4 \cdot 40000$ hr $= 28000$ c.u.

$2000C_3 + 1000 V_3 + 0.4 \cdot 10000$ hr $= 7000$ c.u.

$18000C + 9000 V + 6000 m_1 + 20000$ stp $= 53\,000$ c.u.

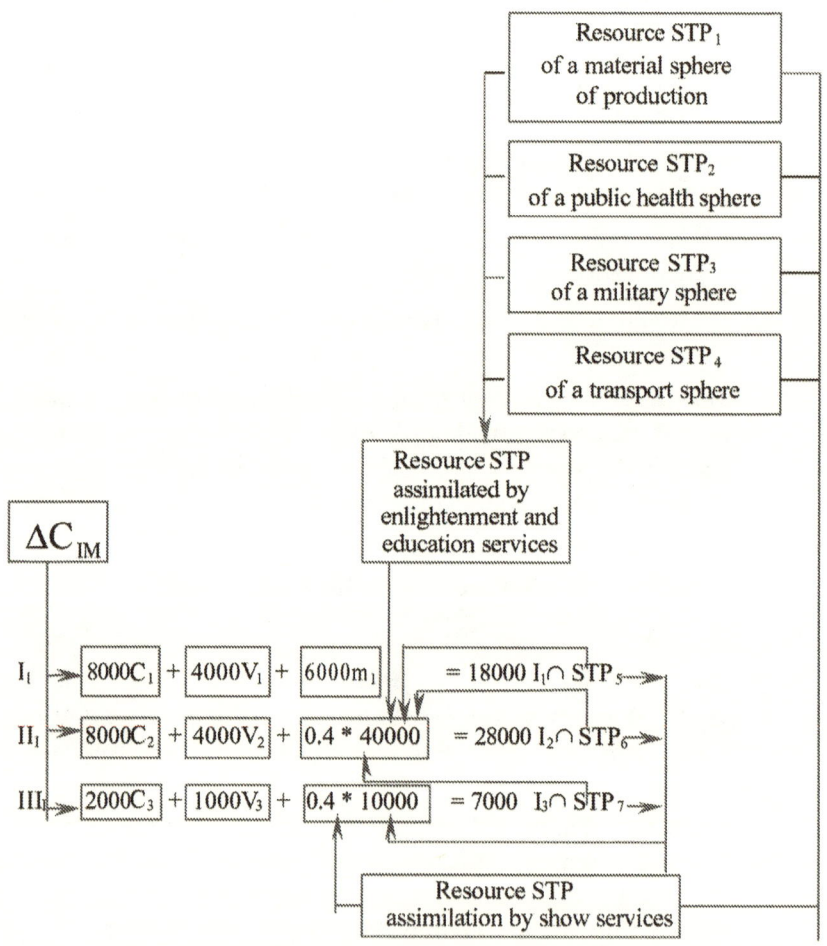

$18000? + 9000V + 6000m_1 + 20000_{STP} = 53000\ I \cap STP$

| Divisions | Indicators of Scheme № 4 | | | | | | % | |
|---|---|---|---|---|---|---|---|---|
| | Inner correlations | | | | | | | |
| I | $C_1$ | 8000 | | | | | | |
| | | $V_1$ | 4000 | $C/V = 2$ | | | | $NI_1$ |
| | | | $m_1$ | $V/m = 2/3$ | | | | |
| | $C_1 + V_1 + m_1$ | | | $m/V = 1.5$ | | | 18000 | $I_1$ |
| | | | | $m/(C+V) = 0.5$ | | | | |
| | | | | $m/(V+m) = 0.6$ | | | | |
| | | | | $(V_1+m_1)/I_1 = 0.55$ | | | | |
| II | Expenses of production of services of education | | $C_2$ | | | | | |
| | | | | $V_2$ | | $C/V = 2$ | | $NI_2$ |
| | Net income | | | | $A^E_{STP}$ | - | $V/A_{STP} = 1/4$ | |
| | | | | | | $A_{STP}/V = 4$ | | |
| | | $C_1 + V_1 + A^E_{STP}$ | | | | | 14000 | $I_2$ |
| | | | | | | $A_{STP}/(C+V) = 4/3$ | | |
| | | | | | | $(V_2 + E_{STP})/I_2 = 0.71$ | | |
| III | | | Production expenses of show services | $C_3$ | | | | |
| | | | | | $V_3$ | | | $NI_3$ |
| | | | Net income | | | $A^{III}_{STP}$ | | |
| | | | | $C_3 + V_3 + A^E_{STP}$ | | | 7000 | $I_3$ |
| | | | | | | | | $I_1/I_2 = 0.64$ |
| | | | | $A^{III}_{STP}/(C_3+V_3) = 4/3$ | | | | $I_2/I_3 = 4$ |
| | | | | $(V_3 + A_{STP})/I_3 = 5/7$ | | | | $(I_2+I_3)/I_1 = 1.94$ |
| $I_1$ | $C_1 + V_1 + m_1$ | | | | | | | |
| $I_2$ | | | $C_2 + V_2 + A^E_{STP}$ | | | | | |
| $I_3$ | | | | $C_3 + V_3 + A^E_{STP}$ | | | | |
| $I_{TOTAL}$ | $18000C + 9000V + 6000m + 20000_{STP}$ | | | | | | 53000 | |

A peculiarity of considered scheme № 4 of the intellectual sphere reproduction lies in a primary development of the «enlightenment» and «education» branches over the «entertainment» branches. The same is expressed as follows:

*First* — past labor expenses $C_1$ (8000) in Division I are equal to the past labor expenses in Division II $C_2$ (8000), and they are four times higher than the past labor expenses in Division III $C_3$ (2000). In other words, the capital assets of the show sphere branches are considerably less developed than the material and technical basis of the «enlightenment», «education» branches;

**_Second_** direct labor expenses in IP Division I $V_1$ (4000) are equal to the direct labor expenses in IP Division II $V_2$ (4000) that are four higher times than the direct labor expenses in the show branches;

**_Third_** as regards the scheme under consideration, a preference in the resource STP assimilation is given to the «enlightenment» and «education» branches, the volume of the «entertainment» services is four times less (28000/7000);

**_Fourth_** the sum of the intellectual services $(I_2 + I_3)$ of «Enlightenment» and «education» (28000) and «entertainment» services (7000) comes to 35000 c.u., and this is about two times more than a volume of the intellectual values produced in IP Division I;

**_Fifth_** the peculiar feature of the inner structure of IP GDP in the reproduction scheme is as follows:

- past labor expenses in Divisions II & III (8000 + 2000) are more by 2000 than past labor expenses in IP Division I (8000 c.u.), past labor expenses in IP Division I come to 15 per cent in the whole volume of GDP;

- direct labor expenses are equal in IP Divisions I & II, and they are four times higher than those of the show branches. This fact reflects a primary development of the «enlightenment» and «education» sub-branches over the «entertainment» one;

- common expenses on creation of IP GDP as against scheme № 4 come to 27000 c.u., and this comes to 51 per cent in the whole volume of IP GDP;

- a volume of the assimilated resource STP comes to 37,7 per cent of IP GDP;

**_Sixth_** a volume of the produced intellectual values coming as pictures, books, newspapers, magazines, etc., is equal to past labor expenses taking place within the intellectual sphere, i.e. $(C_1 + C_2 + C_3)$ = 18000 c.u.

$$I(C + V + m) = IC + IIC + IIIC$$
$$\underbrace{\hspace{3cm}}_{18000} \qquad \underbrace{\hspace{3cm}}_{18000}$$

The equality reflects the fact of a compensation of past labor expenses that take place in the sphere under consideration while producing the intellectual values and services.

$$4000C_1 + 2000\,V_1 + 1000\,m_1 \qquad = 7000 \text{ c.u.}$$
$$2000C_2 + 1000\,V_2 + 0.4 \cdot 10000 \text{ hour.} = 7000 \text{ c.u.}$$
$$4000C_3 + 2000\,V_3 + 0.4 \cdot 20000 \text{ hour.} = 14000 \text{ c.u.}$$
$$\overline{10000C + 5000\,V + 1000\,m_1 + 12000stp = 28\,000 \text{ c.u.}}$$

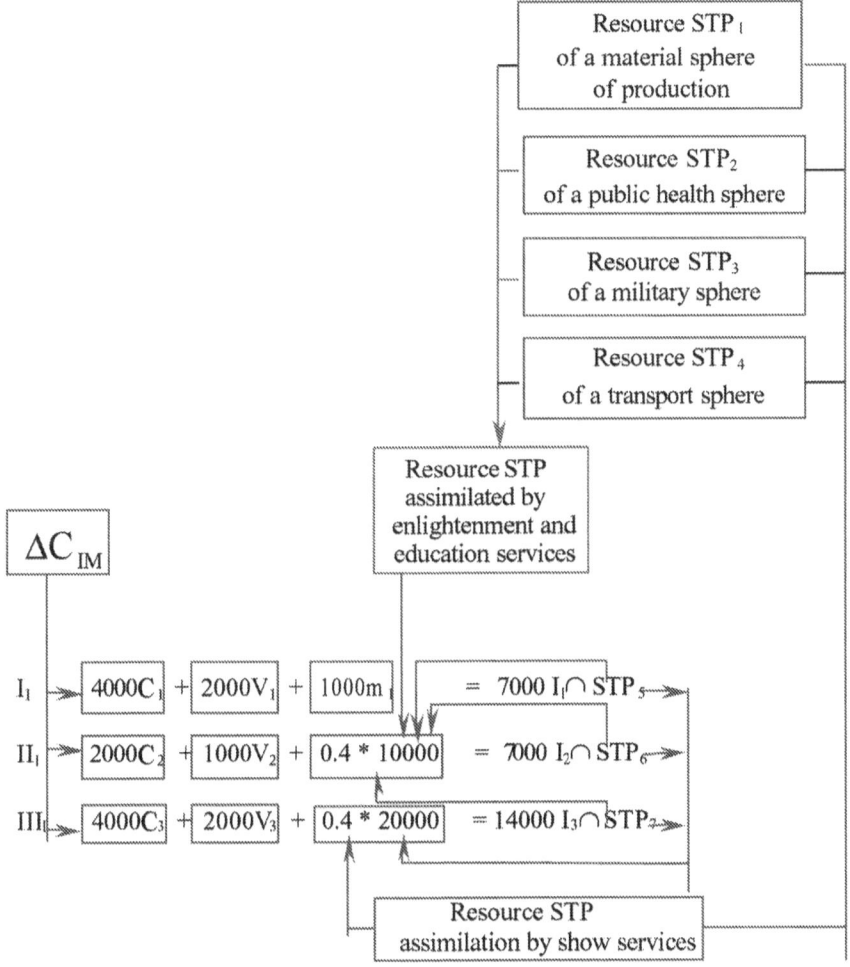

$$10000C + 5000V + 1000m_1 + 12000_{STP} = 28000\ I \cap STP$$

| Divisions | Indicators of Scheme № 5 — Inner correlations | | | % | |
|---|---|---|---|---|---|
| **I** | $C_1$ | | | | |
| | $V_1$ | $C/V = 2$ | | | $NI_1$ |
| | $m_1$ | $V/m = 2$ | | | |
| | $C_1 + V_1 + m_1$ | $m/V = 0.5$ | | 7000 | $I_1$ |
| | | $m/(C+V) = 1/6$ | | | |
| | | $m/(V+m) = 1/6$ | | | |
| | | $(V_1+m_1)/I_1 = 3/7$ | | | |
| **II** | Expenses of production of services of education | $C_2$ | | | |
| | $V_2$ | | $C/V = 2$ | | $NI_2$ |
| | | $A^E_{STP}$ — | $V/A_{STP} = 0.25$ | | |
| | Net income | | $A_{STP}/V = 4$ | | |
| | $C_1 + V_1 + A^E_{STP}$ | | | 7000 | $I_2$ |
| | | | $A_{STP}/(C+V) = 4/3$ | | |
| | | | $(V_2 + E_{STP})/I_2 = 5/7$ | | |
| **III** | Production expenses of show services | $C_3$ | | | |
| | $V_3$ | | | | $NI_3$ |
| | Net income | $A^{III}_{STP}$ | | | |
| | | $C_3 + V_3 + A^E_{STP}$ | | 14000 | $I_3$ |
| | | $A^{III}_{STP}/(C_3 + V_3) = 8/6$ | | | $I_1/I_2 = 1$ |
| | | | | | $I_2/I_3 = 0.5$ |
| | | $(V_3 + A_{STP})/I_3 = 5/7$ | | | $(I_2+I_3)/I_1 = 3$ |
| $I_1$ | $C_1 + V_1 + m_1$ | | | | |
| $I_2$ | | $C_2 + V_2 + A^E_{STP}$ | | | |
| $I_3$ | | | $C_3 + V_3 + A^E_{STP}$ | | |
| $I_{TOTAL}$ | $10000C + 5000V + 1000m + 12000_{STP}$ | | | 28000 | |

A peculiarity of considered scheme №5 of the intellectual sphere reproduction lies in <u>the primary development of show branches over the branches of «Enlightenment», «Education».</u> The above noted is expressed as follows:

*__First,__* summary past labor expenses in «enlightenment» and «education» sub-branches and in «entertainment» branch, $C_2 + C_3 = 2000 + 4000 = 6000$, are higher than those in IP Division I $C_1 = 4000$, besides, past labor expenses in «Entertainment» branch ($C_3$ = 4000) are two times higher than the respecting in «enlightenment», «education» branches ($C_2$ = 2000). In other words, a material and technical basis of the «entertainment» industry is two times higher than that of «enlightenment», «education»;

*Second,* direct labor expenses in the branches producing intellectual values (books, pictures, magazines, newspapers, films, TV sets and Radios), ($V_1$ = 2000), are equal to the direct labor expenses of the entertaining industry ($V_3$ = 2000). At the same time the direct labor expenses of the «enlightenment» and «education» branches are two times less than those of Divisions I & III;

*Third,* as regards the scheme under consideration, a preference in the resource STP assimilation is given to the show branches. The volume of the «entertainment» services granted to people is two times higher than that of the «enlightenment» and «education» services (14000/7000);

*Fourth,* the summary volume of the intellectual services ($D_2$ + $D_3$) comes to 21000 c.u., and this exceeds the intellectual values produced in IP Division I by three times;

*Fifth,* the peculiarity of the inner structure of IP GDP in scheme № 5 is as follows:

- summary expenses of past labor ($C_1$ + $C_2$ + $C_3$) = 10000 C, and the same comes to 35,7 per cent in the volume of IP GDP;
- summary expenses of direct labor, ($V_1$ + $V_2$ + $V_3$) = 5000 V, come to 17,8 per cent in the volume of IP GDP;
- common expenses while creating IP GDP against Scheme C5 come to 53,6 per cent of the volume;
- a volume of the assimilated resource STP comes to 46,4 per cent of IP GDP;

*Sixth,* as regards scheme № 5, the volume of the produced intellectual values (books, pictures, magazines, newspapers, films, TV sets, Radios) is considerably less than the required volume, which is in the intellectual sphere to restore past labor expenses $C_1$, $C_2$, $C_3$, made while creating IP GDP, i.e.

$$I (C + V + m) - (Ic + IIc + IIIc) < 0.$$

The inequality reflects the fact that there is no compensation for past labor expenses in the intellectual process of production.

$4000\,C_1 + 4000\,V_1 + 4000\,m_1\quad = 12000$ c.u.

$2000\,C_2 + 1000\,V_2 + 0.4 \cdot 10000$ hr $= 7000$ c.u.

$6000\,C_3 + 3000\,V_3 + 0.4 \cdot 30000$ hr $= 21000$ c.u.

$12000\,C + 8000\,V + 4000\,m_1 + 16000$ stp $= 40\,000$ c.u.

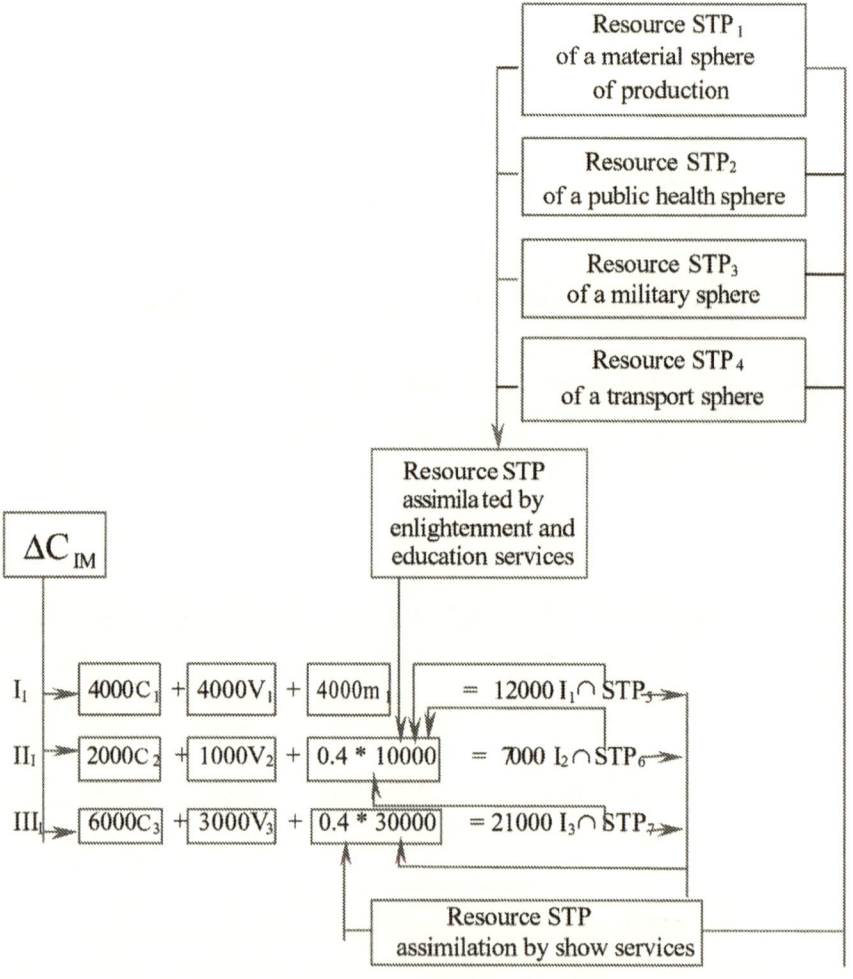

$12000C + 8000V + 4000m_1 + 16000\,{}_{STP} = 40000\ I \cap STP$

| Divisions | Indicators of Scheme № 6 | | | | | | | % | |
|---|---|---|---|---|---|---|---|---|---|
| | Inner correlations | | | | | | | % | |
| **I** | $C_1$ | | | | | | | | |
| | | $V_1$ | | $C/V = 1$ | | | | | $NI_1$ |
| | | | $m_1$ | $V/m = 1$ | | | | | |
| | $C_1 + V_1 + m_1$ | | | $m/V = 1$ | | | | 12000 | $I_1$ |
| | | | | $m/(C+V) = 0.5$ | | | | | |
| | | | | $m/(V+m) = 0.5$ | | | | | |
| | | | | $(V_1+m_1)/I_1 = 1/5$ | | | | | |
| **II** | Expenses of production of services of education | $C_2$ | | | | | | | |
| | | $V_2$ | | | $C/V = 2$ | | | | $NI_2$ |
| | Net income | | $A^E_{STP}$ | - | $V/(m+A_{STP}) = 1/4$ | | | | |
| | | | | | $A_{STP}/V = 4$ | | | | |
| | $C_1 + V_1 + A^E_{STP}$ | | | | | | | 7000 | $I_2$ |
| | | | | | $A_{STP}/(C+V) = 4/3$ | | | | |
| | | | | | $(V_2 + E_{STP})/I_2 = 5/7$ | | | | |
| **III** | Production expenses of show services | | $C_3$ | | | | | | |
| | | | $V_3$ | | | | | | $NI_3$ |
| | Net income | | | $A^{III}_{STP}$ | | | | | |
| | | | $C_3 + V_3 + A^E_{STP}$ | | | | | 21000 | $I_3$ |
| | | | | | | | | | $I_1/I_2 = 1.71$ |
| | | | | $A^{III}_{STP}/(C_3+V_3) = 4/3$ | | | | | $I_2/I_3 = 1/3$ |
| | | | $(V_3 + A_{STP})/I_3 = 0.71$ | | | | | | $(I_2+I_3)/I_1 = 2.33$ |
| $I_1$ | $C_1 + V_1 + m_1$ | | | | | | | | |
| $I_2$ | | $C_2 + V_2 + A^E_{STP}$ | | | | | | | |
| $I_3$ | | | $C_3 + V_3 + A^E_{STP}$ | | | | | | |
| $I_{TOTAL}$ | $12000C + 8000V + 4000m + 16000_{STP}$ | | | | | | | 40000 | |

The proposed variant of the intellectual sphere development (scheme № 6) makes a supposition that the show branches are three times more developed than the «enlightenment», «education» branches. The peculiarity noted is expressed as follows:

*First,*   past labor expenses in the show sphere are three times higher than the same in the «enlightenment» and «education» branches ($6000C_3/2000C_2$);

*Second,* direct labor expenses in the «entertainment branches» are three times higher than the respective expenses in «enlightenment» and «education» ($3000V_3/1000V_2$);

*Third,*   aggregate expenses of the direct and past labor in Division III are three times higher than the same in Division II;

*Fourth,* the volume of the «entertainment» services granted to people by the corresponding branches is three times bigger than a volume of the «enlightenment» and «education» intellectual services (21000 y.e./7000 y.e.);

*Fifth,*   the peculiarity of the inner structure of IP GDP is as follows:

- summary expenses of past labor, $C_1 + C_2 + C_3 = 12000$ c.u., come to 40 per cent of IP GDP;

- summary expenses of direct labor, $V_1 + V_2 + V_3 = 8000V$, come to 20 per cent of IP GDP;

- summary expenses of past and direct labor in IP, against the scheme proposed, come to 50 per cent of IP GDP;

- the volume of the assimilated resource STP comes to 40 per cent of IP GDP;

*Sixth,* as per proposed variant of the reproduction scheme of intellectual sphere, a product of labor of its Division I, $D_1$, is equal to past labor expenses of Divisions I, II & III, i.e.

$$D_1 = \underbrace{IC + IIC + IIIC}$$

$$\underbrace{\phantom{D_1}}_{12000} \quad \underbrace{\phantom{IC + IIC + IIIC}}_{12000}$$

The equality stresses out the fact of a compensation of past labor in the intellectual sphere of production expended by the branches producing material-intellectual values (books, pictures, films, newspapers, magazines, TV sets, Radios, etc.).

*Scheme № 7*

$$4000\ C_1 + 4000\ V_1 + 4000\ m_1 \qquad = 12000\ \text{c.u.}$$

$$2000\ C_2 + 1000\ V_2 + 0.4 \cdot 10000\ \text{hr} \quad = 7000\ \text{c.u.}$$

$$8000\ C_3 + 4000\ V_3 + 0.4 \cdot 40000\ \text{hr} \quad = 28000\ \text{c.u.}$$

$$14000\ C + 9000\ V \quad + 4000\ m_1 + 20000\ \text{stp} = 47\,000\ \text{c.u.}$$

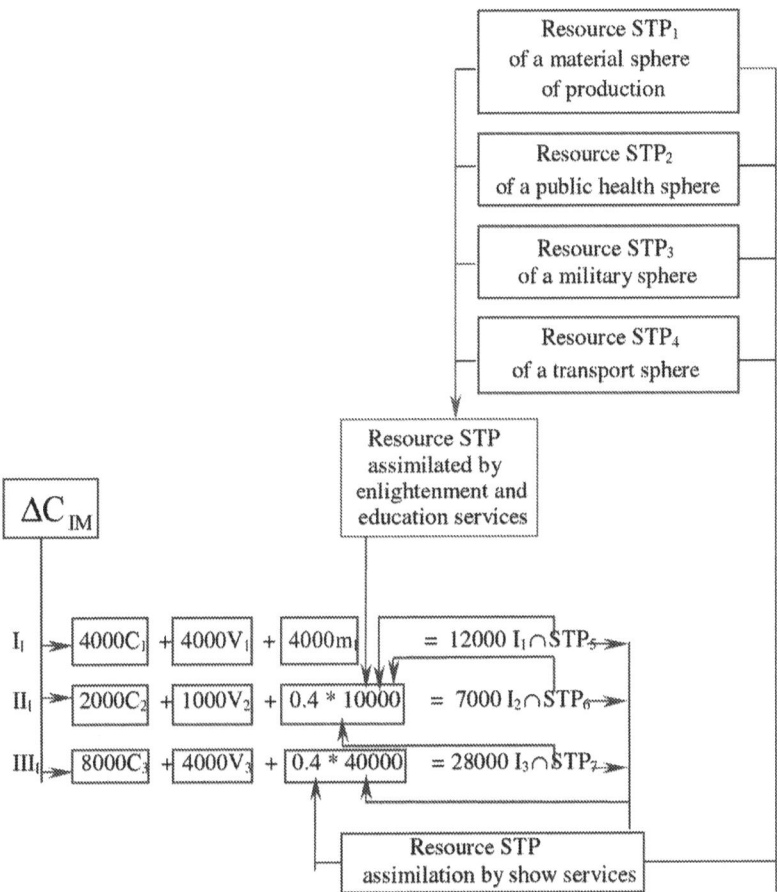

$$14000C + 9000V + 4000m_1 + 20000_{STP} = 47000\ I \cap STP$$

| Divisions | Indicators of Scheme № 7 | | | | |
|---|---|---|---|---|---|
| | Inner correlations | | | | % |
| **I** | $C_1$ | | | | |
| | | $V_1$ | | $C/V = 1$ | | $NI_1$ |
| | | | $m_1$ | $V/m = 1$ | | |
| | $C_1 + V_1 + m_1$ | | | $m/V = 1$ | 12000 | $I_1$ |
| | | | | $m/(C+V) = 0.5$ | | |
| | | | | $m/(V+m) = 0.5$ | | |
| | | | | $(V_1+m_1)/I_1 = 0.66$ | | |
| **II** | Expenses of production of services of education | $C_2$ | | | | |
| | | $V_2$ | | $C/V = 2$ | | $NI_2$ |
| | | | $A^E_{STP}$ | - | $V/(m+A_{STP}) = 1/4$ | |
| | Net income | | | $A_{STP}/V = 1/4$ | | |
| | | $C_1 + V_1 + A^E_{STP}$ | | | 7000 | $I_2$ |
| | | | | $A_{STP}/(C+V) = 4/3$ | | |
| | | | | $(V_2 + E_{STP})/I_2 = 5/7$ | | |
| **III** | Production expenses of show services | $C_3$ | | | | |
| | | $V_3$ | | | | $NI_3$ |
| | Net income | | $A^{III}_{STP}$ | | | |
| | | $C_3 + V_3 + A^E_{STP}$ | | | 28000 | $I_3$ |
| | | $A^{III}_{STP}/(C_3+V_3) = 4/3$ | | | | $I_1/I_2 = 12/7$ |
| | | | | | | $I_2/I_3 = 1/4$ |
| | | $(V_3 + A_{STP})/I_3 = 0.57$ | | | | $(I_2+I_3)/I_1 = 2.9$ |
| $I_1$ | $C_1 + V_1 + m_1$ | | | | | |
| $I_2$ | | $C_2 + V_2 + A^E_{STP}$ | | | | |
| $I_3$ | | | $C_3 + V_3 + A^E_{STP}$ | | | |
| $I_{TOTAL}$ | $14000C + 9000V + 4000m + 20000_{STP}$ | | | | 47000 |

## 3. THE REPRODUCTION OF THE INTELLECTUAL SPHERE IN TERMS OF ASSIMILATED AND PARTIALLY PAID RESOURCE STP

At this stage of the research I will consider the variants of the intellectual sphere reproduction as follows:

*First,* the branches producing books, newspapers, magazines, films, TV sets and Radios do bring some definite income to their producers ($m_1$);

*Second,* a portion of the assimilated resource STP is not paid in «enlighten-ment» and «education»—the intellectual services are consumed free of charge, and another portion of the assimilated resource STP is paid - $m_2$.

*Third,* a portion of the assimilated resource STP is not paid in «entertain-ment» branch—the «entertainment» services are consumed free of charge, and another portion of the assimilated resource STP is paid - $m_3$.

Based on the above, the reproduction scheme of the intellectual sphere is written down as follows:[19]

$$\begin{cases} C_1 + V_1 + m_1 & = D_1 \cap STP \\ C_2 + V_2 + m_2 + UA^{B}_{STP} & = D_2 \cap STP \\ C_3 + V_3 + m_3 + UA^{III}_{STP} & = D_3 \cap STP \end{cases}$$

$$(C_1 + C_2 + C_3) + (V_1 + V_2 + V_3) + (m_1 + m_2 + m_3) + UA^{E}_{STP} + UA^{III}_{STP}$$

, where

$m_2$, $m_3$—a paid portion of the assimilated resource STP;

—an unpaid portion of the assimilated resource STP.

$\cap$ STP_a non-assimilated portion of STP

Several variants of the intellectual production structure may be considered.

---

19    $A^{III}_{STP} = A^{S}_{STP}$, $UA^{E}_{STP} = A^{E}_{STP}$, $UA^{III}_{STP} = A^{S}_{STP}$

## Scheme A

We consider a variant <u>of an excess of direct labor expenses in intellectual sphere</u> <u>Division I</u> that go for the production of the material-intellectual values (books, pictures, films, TV sets, Radios), which are to enter IP Divisions II & III replacing a quitting portion (IIc and IIIc). The material-intellectual values are produced at such an amount that it allows to restore and add a new portion to the quitting material and technical basis of IP Divisions II & III.

$$C_1 + \boxed{V_1 + m_1} = D_1 \cap STP$$

$$\boxed{<}$$

$$\boxed{C_2} + V_2 + m_2 + UA\,{}^{E}_{STP} = D_2 \cap STP$$

$$\boxed{C_3} + V_3 + m_3 + UA\,{}^{S}_{STP} = D_3 \cap STP$$

$$I\,(C_1 + V_1 + m_1) > (Ic + IIc + IIIc) \text{ or}$$

$$I\,(V_1 + m_1) > (IIc + IIIc) \text{ or}$$

$$I\,(V_1 + m_1) - (IIc + IIIc) > 0.$$

As per Scheme A, the product of labor of IP Division I exceeds past labor expenses $C_1 + C_2 + C_3$, which are transferred onto the newly created intellectual values $(D_1)$ and intellectual services of «enlightenment» and «education» $(D_2)$ and «entertainment» services $(D_3)$.

The scheme considers a problem of direct labor expenses in IP Division I $(V_1 + m_1)$ with an amount of investments (of past labor) that go for the creation of the material and technical basis of intellectual production Divisions II & III (IIc + IIIc).

## Scheme B

Direct labor expenses in IP Division I are equal to a quitting portion of past labor in IP Divisions II & III in the reproduction scheme proposed here. In other words, all and everything that has been transferred into the newly created intellectual services of «enlightenment», «education» and «entertainment» services is restored.

$$C_1 + \boxed{V_1 + m_1} = D_1 \cap STP$$

$$\boxed{C_2} + V_2 + m_2 + UA^E_{STP} = D_2 \cap STP$$

$$\boxed{C_3} + V_3 + m_3 + UA^S_{STP} = D_3 \cap STP$$

Scheme B holds the following equalities

$$(C_1 + V_1 + m_1) = C_1 + C_2 + C_3 \text{ or}$$
$$(V_1 + m_1) = (C_2 + C_3).$$

And this means that all past labor expenses spent for the production of the intellectual values and services are compensated within the sphere.

In other words, we are considering the variant of a coincidence of the quitting portion of the material and technical basis of Divisions II & III with a newly created volume of the material-intellectual values of IP Division I.

$$I\,(V_1 + m_1) = (IIc + IIIc) \text{ or}$$
$$I\,(V_1 + m_1) - (IIc + IIIc) = 0.$$

The scheme requires to clarify the correlations, a proportion of the quitting portion (of the past labor) IIc and III$_C$ that are: *first,* the MTB of the second Division is worn out quicker than the MTB of IP Division III. $(C_2 > C_3)$; *second,* the rates of wear of MTB II and MTB III are equal, i.e. $C_2 = C_3$; *third,* the rates of wear of MTB of Division III are higher than the wear rates of MTB of Division II $(C_2 < C_3)$.

## Scheme C

Scheme C reflects a variant of the intellectual sphere functioning when past labor expenses are partially restored in it, i.e. an insufficient amount of the material-intellectual values required for a reproduction is produced within Division I. [20]

$$(C_1 + C_2 + C_3) > D_1 \text{ or}$$
$$(C_2 + C_3) > I(V_1 + m_1)$$

$$C_1 + \boxed{V_1 + m_1} = D_1 \cap STP$$

$$\boxed{>}$$

$$\boxed{C_2} + V_2 + m_2 + UA^E_{STP} = D_2 \cap STP$$

$$\boxed{C_3} + V_3 + m_3 + UA^S_{STP} = D_3 \cap STP$$

Apart from the above, there arise some problems of distribution of the newly created product of IP Division I—$D_1$ between Divisions I, II & III. And three variants appear to be here.

*First,* the material-intellectual values are to be more directed into IP Division II than into «Entertainment» branch .**IIc > IIIc**;

---

20   $UA^E_{STP} = A^E_{STP}$, $UA^{III}_{STP} = A^S_{STP}$

***Second,*** the quantity of the material-intellectual values directed into Divisions II & III is equal, i.e. **IIc = IIIc;**

***Third,*** the quantity of the material-intellectual values directed into Division III exceeds the same directed into Division II, i.e. **IIc < IIIc** .

$C_1$, $C_2$ and $C_3$ are possible to take different values within the above equalities and inequalities:

$C_2$ = $C_3$—past labor of the «enlightenment» and «education» branches and of the «entertainment» branch transferred to the corresponding intellectual services equals.

$C_2$ > $C_3$—a proportion of the past labor transferred in the «enlightenment», «education» branches is more than that in the branches producing «entertainment» services.

$C_2$ < $C_3$—a proportion of the past labor transferred in the «entertainment» branch is more than that of the «enlightenment» and «education» branches.

$$2000\ C_1 + 1000\ V_1 + 1000m_1 \qquad\qquad\qquad = 4000\ \text{c.u.}$$
$$2000\ C_2 + 1000\ V_2 + 1000m_2 + 0.4 \cdot 10000\ \text{hr} = 8000\ \text{c.u.}$$
$$\underline{2000\ C_3 + 1000\ V_3 + 1000m_3 + 0.4 \cdot 10000\ \text{hr} = 8000\ \text{c.u.}}$$
$$6000\ C + 3000\ V \quad + 3000\ m + 8000\ \text{stp} \qquad = 20\ 000\ \text{c.u.}\ ^{21}$$

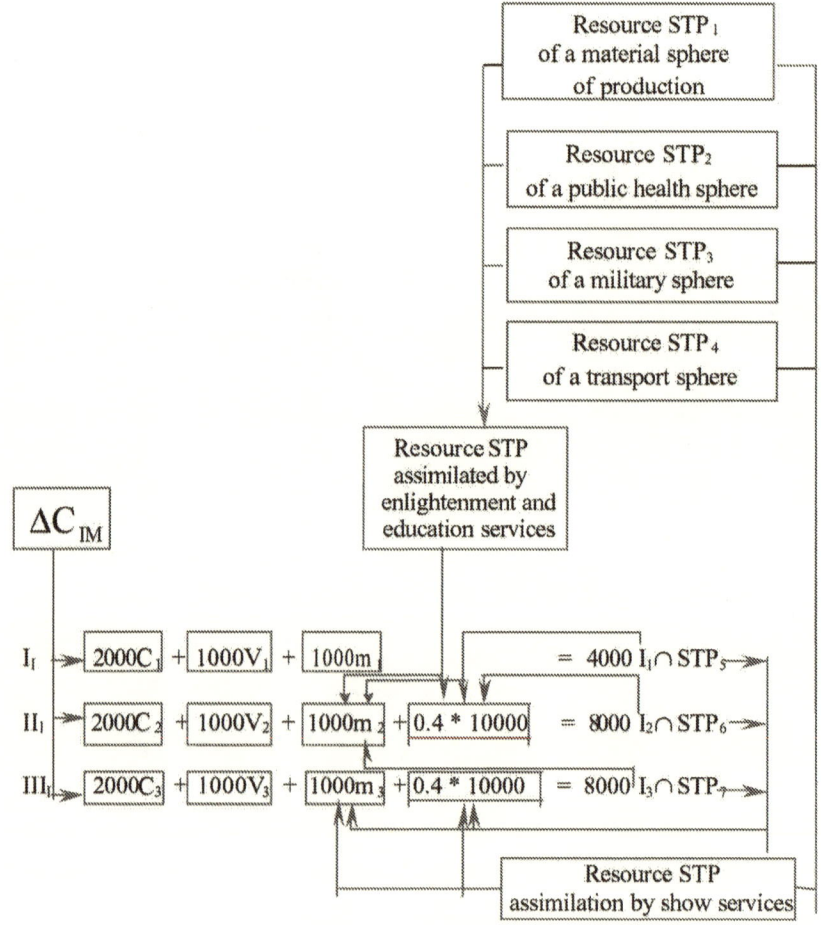

$$6000\text{C} + 3000\text{V} + 3000\text{m}_{\text{l}} + 8000_{\text{STP}} = 20000\ \text{I} \cap \text{STP}$$

---

21   $4000 + 4000 = 8000_{STP}$ - an assimilated but unpaid portion of resource STP.

| Divisions | Indicators of Scheme № 8 | | | | | |
|---|---|---|---|---|---|---|
| | Inner correlations | | | | | % |
| **I** | $C_1$ 2000 | | | | | |
| | | $V_1$ 1000 | $C/V = 2$ | | | |
| | | $m_1$ | $V/m = 1$ | | | $NI_1$ |
| | $C_1+V_1+m_1$ | | $m/V = 1$ | | 4000 | $I_1$ |
| | | | $m/(C+V) = 1/3$ | | | |
| | | | $m/(V+m) = 1/2$ | | | |
| | | | $(V_1+m_1)/I_1 = 1/2$ | | | |
| **II** | Expenses of production of services of education | $C_2$ 2000 | | | | |
| | | $V_2$ 1000 | $C/V = 2$ | | | |
| | Net income | $m_2$ 1000 | $V/(m+A_{STP}) = 1/5$ | | | $NI_2$ |
| | | $A^E_{STP}$ | $4000(m+A^E_{STP})/V = 5$ | | | |
| | $C_1+V_1+m_1+A^E_{STP}$ | | $8000$ | | | $I_2$ |
| | | | $(m+A^E_{STP})/(C+V) = 5/3$ | | | |
| | | | $A^E_{STP}/(C+V) = 4/3$ | | | |
| | | | $(V_2+m_2+A^E_{STP})/I_2 = 3/4$ | | | |
| **III** | Production expenses of show services | $C_3$ 2000 | | | | |
| | | $V_3$ 1000 | $2C/V$ | | | |
| | Net income | $m_3$ 1000 | | | | $NI_3$ |
| | | $A^{III}_{STP}$ | | 4000 | | |
| | $C_3+V_3+m_3+A^E_{STP}$ | | 8000 | | | $I_3$ |
| | | | $(m+A_{STP})/(C+V)=5/3$ | | | $I_1/I_2=½$ |
| | | | $A_{STP}/(C_3+V_3)=4/3$ | | | $I_2/I_3=1$ |
| | | | $(V_3+m_3+A_{STP})/I_3=3/4$ | | | $(I_2+I_3)/I_1=4$ |
| $I_1$ | $C_1+V_1+m_1$ | | | | | |
| $I_2$ | $C_2+V_2+m_2+A^E_{STP}$ | | | | | |
| $I_3$ | $C_3+V_3+m_3+A^E_{STP}$ | | | | | |
| $I_{TOTAL}$ | $6000C+3000V+3000m+8000_{STP}$ | | | | | 20000 |

$$4000\ C_1 + 1000\ V_1 + 1000m_1 \qquad\qquad = 6000\ \text{c.u.}$$
$$4000\ C_2 + 2000\ V_2 + 2000m_2 + 0.4 \cdot 20000\ \text{hr} = 16000\ \text{c.u.}$$
$$\underline{2000\ C_3 + 1000\ V_3 + 1000m_3 + 0.4 \cdot 10000\ \text{hr} = 8000\ \text{c.u.}}$$
$$10000\ \text{C} + 4000\ \text{V} + 4000\ \text{m} + 12000\ \text{stp} = 30\,000\ \text{c.u.}^{22}$$

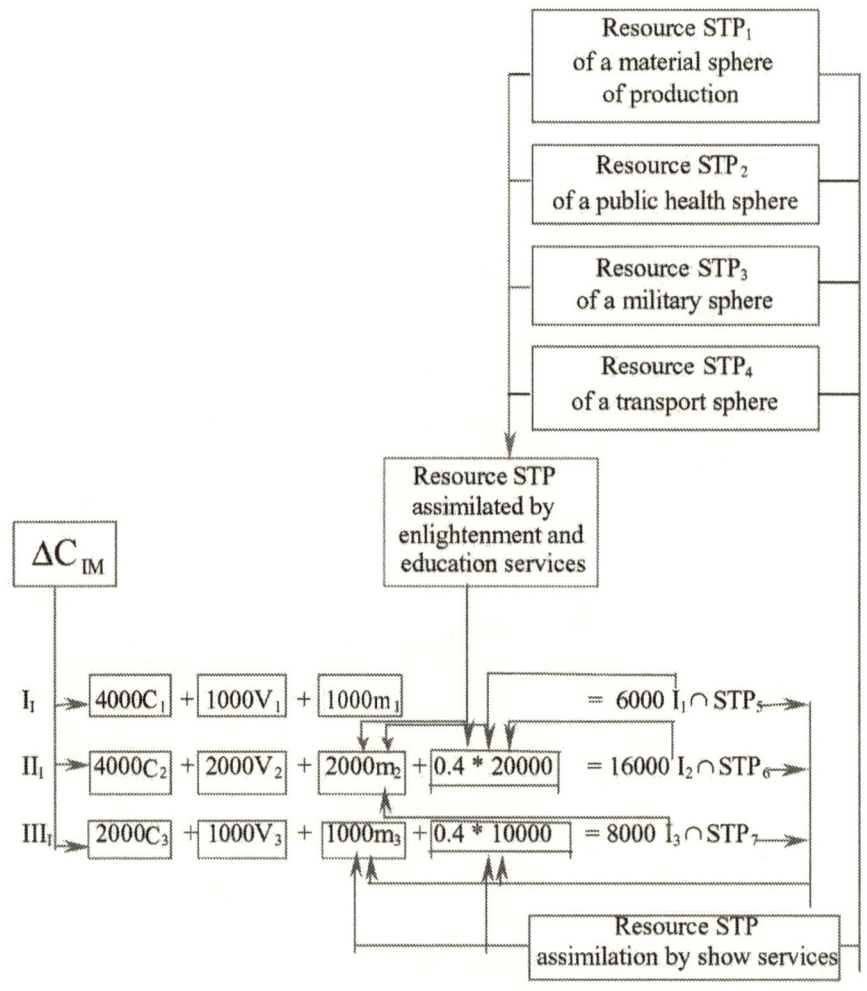

$$10000\text{C} + 4000\text{V} + 4000m_1 + 12000_{STP} = 30000\ \text{I} \cap \text{STP}$$

---

22   $C_2 > C_3,\ V_2 > V_3,\ m_2 > m_3,\ UA^E_{STP} > UA^{III}_{STP}$

| Divisions | Indicators of Scheme № 9 | | | | | | |
|---|---|---|---|---|---|---|---|
| | Inner correlations | | | | | | % |
| **I** | $C_1$ | 4000 | | | | | |
| | | $V_1$ | 1000 | C/V = **4** | | | $NI_1$ |
| | | | $m_1$ | V/m = **1** | | | |
| | $C_1 + V_1 + m_1$ | | | m/V = **1** | 6000 | | $I_1$ |
| | | | | m/(C+V) = **1/5** | | | |
| | | | | m/(V+m) = **1/2** | | | |
| | | | | $(V_1+m_1)/I_1$ = **1/3** | | | |
| **II** | Expenses of production of services of education | $C_2$ | 4000 | | | | |
| | | $V_2$ | 2000 | C/V = **2** | | | $NI_2$ |
| | Net income | | $m_2$ | 2000 | $V/(m+A_{STP})$ = **1/5** | | |
| | | | | $A^E_{STP}$ | $4000(m+A^E_{STP})/V$ = **5** | | |
| | $C_2 + V_2 + m_2 + A^E_{STP}$ | | | | 8000 | | $I_2$ |
| | | | | $(m+A^E_{STP})/(C+V)$ = **5/3** | | | |
| | | | | $A^E_{STP}/(C+V)$ = **4/3** | | | |
| | | | | $(V_2+m_2+A^E_{STP})/I_2$ = **3/4** | | | |
| **III** | Production expenses of show services | $C_3$ | 2000 | | | | |
| | | $V_3$ | 1000 | 2C/V | | | $NI_3$ |
| | | | $m_3$ | 1000 | | | |
| | Net income | | | $A^{III}_{STP}$ | 4000 | | |
| | $C_3 + V_3 + m_3 + A^E_{STP}$ | | | | 8000 | | $I_3$ |
| | $(m+A_{STP})/(C+V_1$ = **5/3** | | | | | | $I_1/I_2$ = **3/8** |
| | $A_{STP}/(C_3+V_3)$ = **4/3** | | | | | | $I_2/I_3$ = **2** |
| | $(V_3+m_3+A_{STP})/I_3$ = **3/4** | | | | | | $(I_2+I_3)/I_1$ = **4** |
| $I_1$ | $C_1 + V_1 + m_1$ | | | | | | |
| $I_2$ | | $C_2 + V_2 + m_2 + A^E_{STP}$ | | | | | |
| $I_3$ | | | $C_3 + V_3 + m_3 + A^E_{STP}$ | | | | |
| $I_{TOTAL}$ | $10000C + 4000V + 4000m + 12000_{STP}$ | | | | | | 30000 |

$$4000\ C_1 + 1000\ V_1 + 1000m_1 \qquad\qquad = 6000\ \text{c.u.}$$

$$6000\ C_2 + 3000\ V_2 + 3000m_2 + 0.4 \cdot 30000\ \text{hr} = 24000\ \text{c.u.}$$

$$\underline{2000\ C_3 + 1000\ V_3 + 1000m_3 + 0.4 \cdot 10000\ \text{hr} = 8000\ \text{c.u.}}$$

$$12000\ C + 5000\ V + 5000\ m + 16000\ \text{stp} \qquad = 38\ 000\ \text{c.u.}^{23}$$

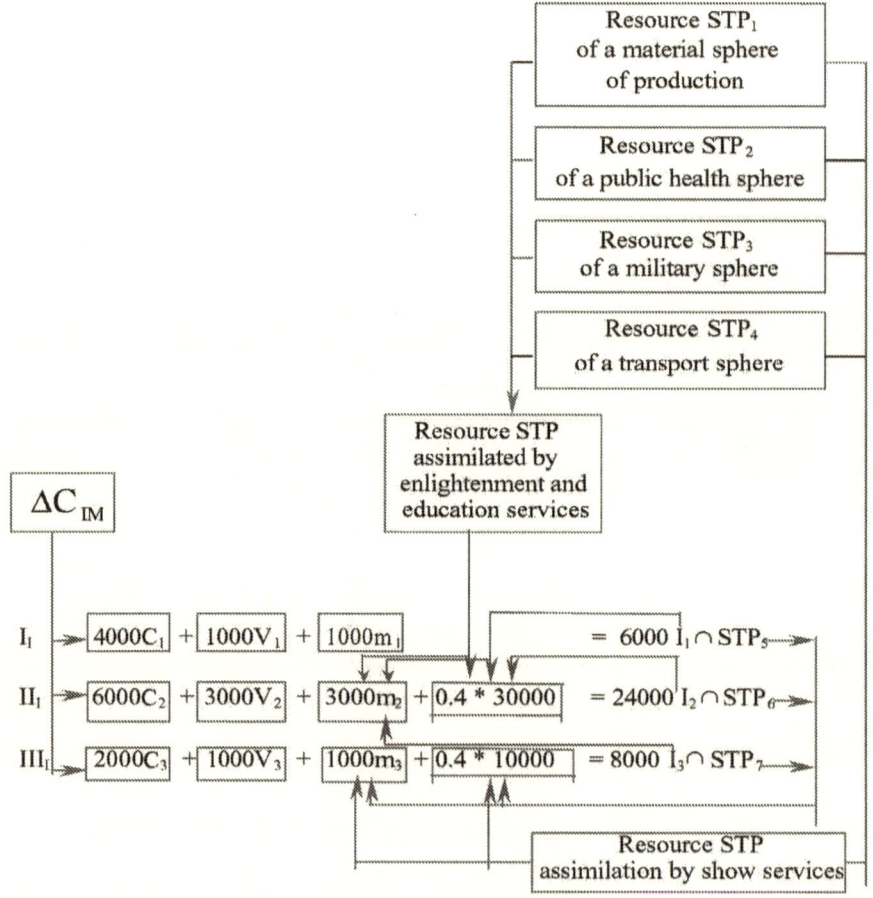

$$12000C + 5000V + 5000m_1 + 16000_{STP} = 38000\ I \cap STP$$

---

23   $C_2 = 3C_3,\ V_2 = 3V_3,\ m_2 = 3m_3,\ UA^E_{STP} > UA^{III}_{STP}$

$3000m_2$ , $1000m_3$ - a paid portion of the assimilated resource STP by "enlighten-ment" and "education" branches and by «Entertainment» branch

| Divisions | Indicators of Scheme № 10 | | | | | | |
|---|---|---|---|---|---|---|---|
| | Inner correlations | | | | | | % |
| I | $C_1$ | 4000 | | | | | |
| | | $V_1$ | 1000 | $C/V = 4$ | | | $NI_1$ |
| | | | $m_1$ | $V/m = 1$ | | | |
| | $C_1 + V_1 + m_1$ | | | $m/V = 1$ | 6000 | | $I_1$ |
| | | | | $m/(C+V) = 1/5$ | | | |
| | | | | $m/(V+m) = 1/2$ | | | |
| | | | | $(V_1+m_1)/I_1 = 1/3$ | | | |
| II | Expenses of production of services of education | $C_2$ | 6000 | | | | $NI_2$ |
| | | $V_2$ | 3000 | $C/V = 2$ | | | |
| | Net income | | $m_2$ | 3000 | $V/(m + A_{STP}) = 1/5$ | | |
| | | | $A^E_{STP}$ | $4000(m + A^E_{STP})/V = 5$ | | | |
| | | $C_1 + V_1 + m_1 + A^E_{STP}$ | | 24000 | | | $I_2$ |
| | | | | $(m + A^E_{STP})/(C+V) = 5/3$ | | | |
| | | | | $A^E_{STP}/(C+V) = 4/3$ | | | |
| | | | | $(V_2 + m_2 + A^E_{STP})/I_2 = 3/4$ | | | |
| III | Production expenses of show services | $C_3$ | 2000 | | | | $NI_3$ |
| | | $V_3$ | 1000 | $2C/V$ | | | |
| | Net income | | $m_3$ | 1000 | | | |
| | | | $A^{III}_{STP}$ | 4000 | | | |
| | | $C_3 + V_3 + m_3 + A^E_{STP}$ | | 8000 | | | $I_3$ |
| | | | | $(m + A_{STP})/(C+V) = 5/3$ | | | $I_1/I_2 = 1/4$ |
| | | | | $A_{STP}/(C_3+V_3) = 4/3$ | | | $I_2/I_3 = 3$ |
| | | | | $(V_3 + m_3 + A_{STP})/I_3 = 3/4$ | | | $(I_2+I_3)/I_1 = 8$ |
| $I_1$ | $C_1 + V_1 + m_1$ | | | | | | |
| $I_2$ | | $C_2 + V_2 + m_2 + A^E_{STP}$ | | | | | |
| $I_3$ | | | $C_3 + V_3 + m_3 + A^E_{STP}$ | | | | |
| $I_{TOTAL}$ | $12000C + 5000V + 5000m + 16000_{STP}$ | | | | | | 38000 |

$$4000\ C_1 + 1000\ V_1 + 1000m_1 \qquad\qquad = 6000\ \text{c.u.}$$

$$8000\ C_2 + 4000\ V_2 + 4000m_2 + 0.4 \cdot 40000\ \text{hr} = 32000\ \text{c.u.}$$

$$\underline{2000\ C_3 + 1000\ V_3 + 1000m_3 + 0.4 \cdot 10000\ \text{hr} = 8000\ \text{c.u.}}$$

$$14000\ C + 6000\ V\ \ + 6000\ m + 20000\ \text{stp}\ \ \ = 46\,000\ \text{c.u.}^{24}$$

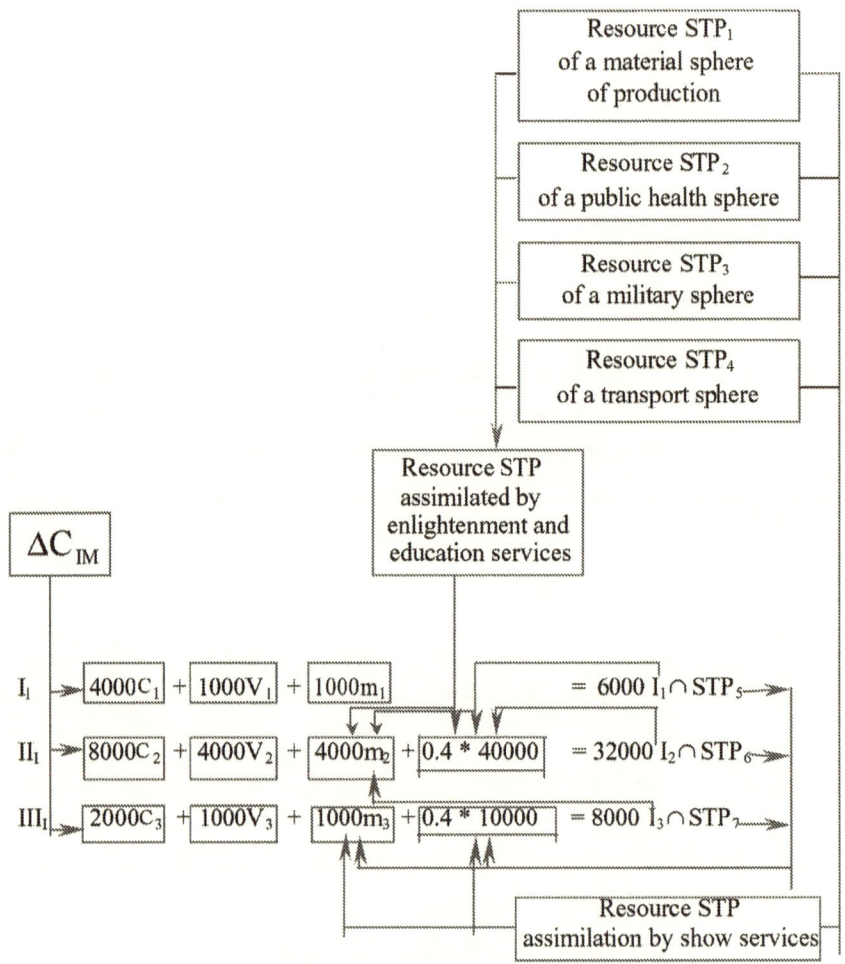

$$14000C + 6000V + 6000m_1 + 20000_{STP} = 46000\ I \cap STP$$

---

24   $C_2 = 4C_3,\ V_2 = 4V_3,\ m_2 = 4m_3,\ UA^{E}_{STP} > UA^{III}_{STP}$

| Divisions | Indicators of Scheme № 11 | | | | | | % |
|---|---|---|---|---|---|---|---|
| | **Inner correlations** | | | | | | **%** |
| **I** | $C_1$ | 4000 | | | | | |
| | | $V_1$ | 1000 | $C/V = 4$ | | | $NI_1$ |
| | | | $m_1$ | $V/m = 1$ | | | |
| | $C_1 + V_1 + m_1$ | | | $m/V = 1$ | 6000 | | $I_1$ |
| | | | | $m/(C+V) = 1/5$ | | | |
| | | | | $m/(V+m) = 1/2$ | | | |
| | | | | $(V_1+m_1)/I_1 = 1/3$ | | | |
| **II** | Expenses of production of services of education | $C_2$ | 8000 | | | | |
| | | | $V_2$ | 4000 | $C/V = 2$ | | $NI_2$ |
| | Net income | | $m_2$ | 4000 | $V/(m + A_{STP}) = 1/5$ | | |
| | | | | $A^E_{STP}$ | $4000(m + A^E_{STP})/V = 5$ | | |
| | | $C_1 + V_1 + m_1 + A^E_{STP}$ | | | 32000 | | $I_2$ |
| | | | | | $(m + A^E_{STP})/(C+V) = 5/3$ | | |
| | | | | | $A^E_{STP}/(C+V) = 4/3$ | | |
| | | | | | $(V_2 + m_2 + A^E_{STP})/I_2 = 3/4$ | | |
| **III** | Production expenses of show services | $C_3$ | 2000 | | | | |
| | | | $V_3$ | 1000 | $2C/V$ | | $NI_3$ |
| | Net income | | $m_3$ | 1000 | | | |
| | | | | $A^{III}_{STP}$ | 4000 | | |
| | | $C_3 + V_3 + m_3 + A^E_{STP}$ | | | 8000 | | $I_3$ |
| | | $(m + A_{STP})/(C+V_3 = 5/3$ | | | | | $I_1/I_2 = 3/16$ |
| | | $A_{STP}/(C_3+V_3) = 4/3$ | | | | | $I_2/I_3 = 4$ |
| | | $(V_3 + m_3 + A_{STP})/I_3 = 3/4$ | | | | | $(I_2+I_3)/I_1 = 20/3$ |
| $I_1$ | $C_1 + V_1 + m_1$ | | | | | | |
| $I_2$ | | $C_2 + V_2 + m_2 + A^E_{STP}$ | | | | | |
| $I_3$ | | $C_3 + V_3 + m_3 + A^E_{STP}$ | | | | | |
| $I_{TOTAL}$ | $14000C + 6000V + 6000m + 20000_{STP}$ | | | | | | 46000 |

**Variant $D_3 > D_2$.** As in the considered variant of the reproduction schemes, the factors participating in the production of «entertainment» service production are two to four times higher than those of the «enlightenment» and «education» services. Such a proportion takes place in the countries whose economy is tourist oriented.

2 times  a) $C_3 = 2 C_2$ , $V_3 = 2 V_2$, $m_3 = 2 m_2$, ; (Scheme 12)

3 times  b) $C_3 = 3 C_2$ , $V_3 = 3 V_2$, $m_3 = 3 m_2$, ; (Scheme 13)

4 times  c) $C_3 = 4C_2$ , $V_3 = 4 V_2$, $m_3 = 4 m_2$, ; (Scheme 14)

$$4000 \ C_1 + 1000 \ V_1 + 1000m_1 \qquad\qquad\qquad = 6000 \ \text{c.u.}$$

$$2000 \ C_2 + 1000 \ V_2 + 1000m_2 + 0.4 \cdot 10000 \ \text{hr} = 8000 \ \text{c.u.}$$

$$\underline{4000 \ C_3 + 2000 \ V_3 + 2000m_3 + 0.4 \cdot 20000 \ \text{hr} = 16000 \ \text{c.u.}}$$

$$10000 \ C + 4000 \ V \ + 4000 \ m + 12000 \ \text{stp} \qquad = 30\,000 \ \text{c.u.}$$

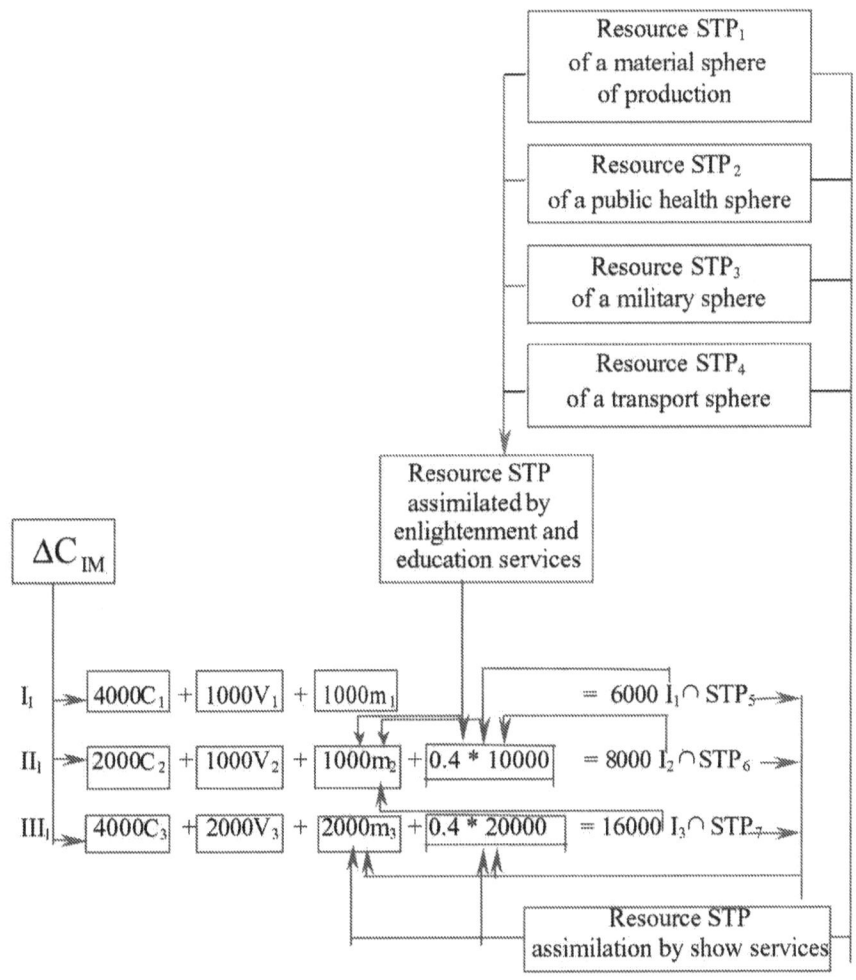

$$10000C + 4000V + 4000m_1 + 12000_{STP} = 30000 \ I \cap STP$$

| Divisions | Indicators of Scheme № 12 | | % |
|---|---|---|---|
| | **Inner correlations** | | |
| **I** | $C_1$  4000 | | |
| | $V_1$  1000     C/V = **4** | | NI$_1$ |
| | $m_1$     V/m = **1** | | |
| | $C_1 + V_1 + m_1$     m/V = **1** | 6000 | I$_1$ |
| | m/(C+V) = **1/5** | | |
| | m/(V+m) = **1/2** | | |
| | $(V_1+m_1)/I_1$ = **1/3** | | |
| **II** | Expenses of production of services of education   $C_2$  2000 | | NI$_2$ |
| | $V_2$  1000     C/V = **2** | | |
| | Net income   $m_2$  1000   V/(m+A$_{STP}$) = **1/5** | | |
| | $A^E_{STP}$   4000(m+A$^E_{STP}$)/V = **5** | | |
| | $C_1 + V_1 + m_1 + A^E_{STP}$ | 8000 | I$_2$ |
| | $(m+A^E_{STP})/(C+V)$ = **5/3** | | |
| | $A^E_{STP}/(C+V)$ = **4/3** | | |
| | $(V_2 + m_2 + A^E_{STP})/I_2$ = **3/4** | | |
| **III** | Production expenses of show services   $C_3$  4000 | | NI$_3$ |
| | $V_3$  2000  2C/V | | |
| | Net income   $m_3$  2000 | | |
| | $A^{III}_{STP}$  8000 | | |
| | $C_3 + V_3 + m_3 + A^E_{STP}$ | 16000 | I$_3$ |
| | $(m + A_{STP})/(C+V)$= **5/3** | | I$_1$/I$_2$ = **3/4** |
| | $A_{STP}/(C_3+V_3)$ = **4/3** | | I$_2$/I$_3$ = **1/2** |
| | $(V_3 + m_3 + A_{STP})/I_3$= **3/4** | | (I$_2$+I$_3$)/I$_1$ = **4** |
| I$_1$ | $C_1 + V_1 + m_1$ | | |
| I$_2$ | $C_2 + V_2 + m_2 + A^E_{STP}$ | | |
| I$_3$ | $C_3 + V_3 + m_3 + A^E_{STP}$ | | |
| I$_{TOTAL}$ | 10000C + 4000V + 4000m + 12000$_{STP}$ | | 30000 |

$$4000\ C_1 + 1000\ V_1 + 1000 m_1 \qquad\qquad\qquad = 6000\ \text{c.u.}$$
$$2000\ C_2 + 1000\ V_2 + 1000 m_2 + 0.4 \cdot 10000\ \text{hr} = 8000\ \text{c.u.}$$
$$\underline{6000\ C_3 + 3000\ V_3 + 3000 m_3 + 0.4 \cdot 30000\ \text{hr} = 24000\ \text{c.u.}}$$
$$12000\ C + 5000\ V \quad + 5000\ m + 16000\ \text{stp} \quad = 38\,000\ \text{c.u.}$$

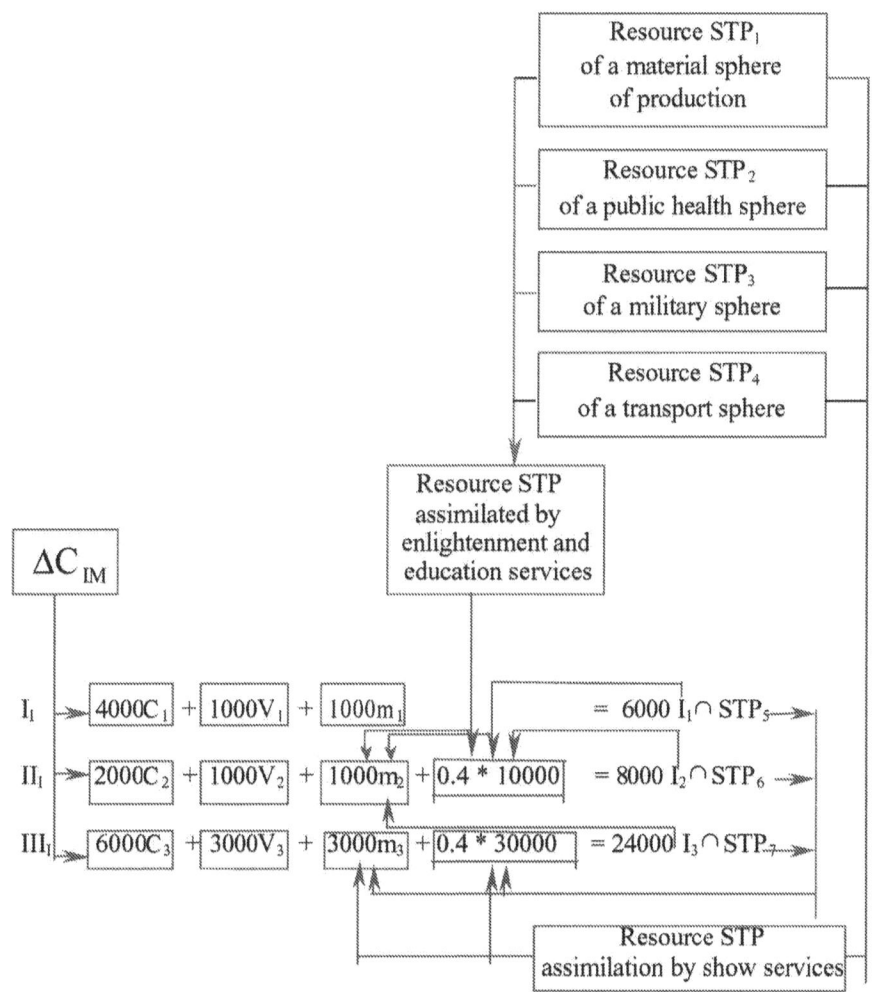

$$12000 C + 5000 V + 5000 m_1 + 16000_{STP} = 38000\ I \cap STP$$

| Divisions | Indicators of Scheme № 13 | | | | | | | % |
|---|---|---|---|---|---|---|---|---|
| | Inner correlations | | | | | | | |
| **I** | $C_1$ | 4000 | | | | | | |
| | | $V_1$ | 1000 | $C/V = 4$ | | | | $NI_1$ |
| | | | $m_1$ | $V/m = 1$ | | | | |
| | $C_1 + V_1 + m_1$ | | | $m/V = 1$ | | 6000 | | $I_1$ |
| | | | | $m/(C+V) = 1/5$ | | | | |
| | | | | $m/(V+m) = 1/2$ | | | | |
| | | | | $(V_1+m_1)/I_1 = 1/3$ | | | | |
| **II** | Expenses of production of services of education | $C_2$ | 2000 | | | | | |
| | | | $V_2$ | 1000 | $C/V = 2$ | | | $NI_2$ |
| | Net income | | | $m_2$ | 1000 | $V/(m + A_{STP}) = 1/5$ | | |
| | | | | | $A^E_{STP}$ | $4000 (m + A^E_{STP})/V = 5$ | | |
| | | $C_1 + V_1 + m_1 + A^E_{STP}$ | | | | 8000 | | $I_2$ |
| | | | | $(m + A^E_{STP})/(C+V) = 5/3$ | | | | |
| | | | | $A^E_{STP}/(C+V) = 4/3$ | | | | |
| | | | | $(V_2 + m_2 + A^E_{STP})/I_2 = 3/4$ | | | | |
| **III** | Production expenses of show services | | $C_3$ | 6000 | | | | |
| | | | | $V_3$ | 3000 | $2C/V$ | | $NI_3$ |
| | Net income | | | | $m_3$ | 3000 | | |
| | | | | | | $A^{III}_{STP}$ | 12000 | |
| | | | $C_3 + V_3 + m_3 + A^E_{STP}$ | | | 24000 | | $I_3$ |
| | | | $(m + A_{STP})/(C+V) = 5/3$ | | | | | $I_1/I_2 = 3/4$ |
| | | | $A_{STP}/(C_3+V_3) = 4/3$ | | | | | $I_2/I_3 = 1/3$ |
| | | | $(V_3 + m_3 + A_{STP})/I_3 = 3/4$ | | | | | $(I_2+I_3)/I_1 = 16/3$ |
| $I_1$ | $C_1 + V_1 + m_1$ | | | | | | | |
| $I_2$ | $C_2 + V_2 + m_2 + A^E_{STP}$ | | | | | | | |
| $I_3$ | $C_3 + V_3 + m_3 + A^E_{STP}$ | | | | | | | |
| $I_{TOTAL}$ | $12000C + 5000V + 5000m + 16000_{STP}$ | | | | | | | 38000 |

*Scheme № 14*

$$4000\ C_1 + 1000\ V_1 + 1000m_1 \qquad\qquad = 6000\ \text{c.u.}$$
$$2000\ C_2 + 1000\ V_2 + 1000m_2 + 0.4 \cdot 10000\ \text{hr} = 8000\ \text{c.u.}$$
$$8000\ C_3 + 4000\ V_3 + 4000m_3 + 0.4 \cdot 40000\ \text{hr} = 32000\ \text{c.u.}$$
$$\overline{14000\ C + 6000\ V\ \ \ + 6000\ m + 20000\ \text{stp} \qquad = 46\ 000\ \text{c.u.}}$$

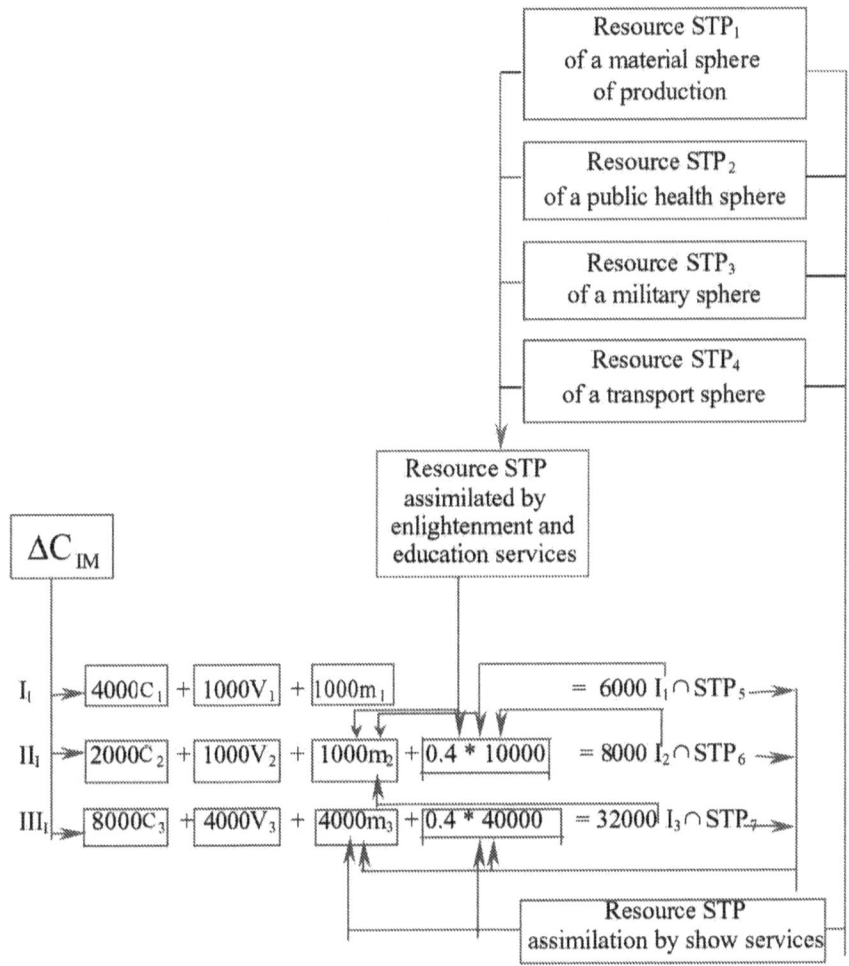

$$14000_C + 6000V + 6000m_1 + 20000_{STP} = 46000\ I \cap STP$$

| Divisions | Indicators of Scheme № 14 | | | | | | | % |
|---|---|---|---|---|---|---|---|---|
| | Inner correlations | | | | | | | % |
| **I** | $C_1$ | 4000 | | | | | | |
| | | $V_1$ | 1000 | $C/V = 4$ | | | | $NI_1$ |
| | | | $m_1$ | $V/m = 1$ | | | | |
| | $C_1 + V_1 + m_1$ | | | $m/V = 1$ | | 6000 | | $I_1$ |
| | | | | $m/(C+V) = 1/5$ | | | | |
| | | | | $m/(V+m) = 1/2$ | | | | |
| | | | | $(V_1+m_1)/I_1 = 1/3$ | | | | |
| **II** | Expenses of production of services of education | $C_2$ | 2000 | | | | | |
| | | | $V_2$ | 1000 | $C/V = 2$ | | | $NI_2$ |
| | | | | $m_2$ | 1000 | $V/(m + A_{STP}) = 1/5$ | | |
| | Net income | | | | $A^E_{STP}$ | $4000(m + A^E_{STP})/V = 5$ | | |
| | $C_1 + V_1 + m_1 + A^E_{STP}$ | | | | | 8000 | | $I_2$ |
| | | | | | $(m + A^E_{STP})/(C+V) = 5/3$ | | | |
| | | | | | $A^E_{STP}/(C+V) = 4/3$ | | | |
| | | | | | $(V_2 + m_2 + A^E_{STP})/I_2 = 3/4$ | | | |
| **III** | Production expenses of show services | $C_3$ | 8000 | | | | | |
| | | | $V_3$ | 4000 | $2C/V$ | | | $NI_3$ |
| | Net income | | | $m_3$ | 4000 | | | |
| | | | | | $A^{III}_{STP}$ | 16000 | | |
| | $C_3 + V_3 + m_3 + A^E_{STP}$ | | | | | 32000 | | $I_3$ |
| | | | | | $(m + A_{STP})/(C+V_3) = 5/3$ | | | $I_1/I_2 = 3/4$ |
| | | | | | $A_{STP}/(C_3+V_3) = 4/3$ | | | $I_2/I_3 = 1/4$ |
| | | | | | $(V_3 + m_3 + A_{STP})/I_3 = 3/4$ | | | $(I_2+I_3)/I_1 = 20/3$ |
| $I_1$ | $C_1 + V_1 + m_1$ | | | | | | | |
| $I_2$ | | | $C_2 + V_2 + m_2 + A^E_{STP}$ | | | | | |
| $I_3$ | | | | | $C_3 + V_3 + m_3 + A^E_{STP}$ | | | |
| $I_{TOTAL}$ | $14000C + 6000V + 6000m + 20000_{STP}$ | | | | | | | 46000 |

## D, E, L VARIANTS
### (reproduction of intellectual sphere)

Together with the above, it is necessary to consider other correlations in the reproduction schemes. Distribution $D_1$ is to be linked with the resource STP, on one hand, assimilated by «enlightenment» and «education» branches and, on the other hand, assimilated by the «Entertainment» branch.

**D. Variant** of a reproduction scheme of the intellectual sphere

$$D_1 = D_2 + D_3 \text{ or}$$

, whereat

$D_1$—the volume of the intellectual values created in intellectual production Division I per annum;

$D_2$—the volume of the intellectual services created in «Enlightenment» and «Education» branches per annum accounting for the resource of population's spare time assimilated by them;

$D_3$—the volume of the intellectual services created in «Entertainment» branch per annum accounting for the assimilated resource of spare time of population.

**D. Variant** of a reproduction scheme of the intellectual sphere

$$D_1 < [D_2 + D_3]$$

It is possible to execute a reduction in the components of the right and left parts, but the following problem arises:

1. if we maintain the expenses on assimilation of the population spare time resource by «enlightenment», «education» and «entertainment» branches, there is no foundation to exclude an unpaid portion of the resource STP out of the equality.

2.  if we exclude an unpaid portion of the resource STP, we decrease a value of GDP and NI. In this case the reproduction schemes of the intellectual sphere would be truncated:

$$[I(V_1 + m_1) + II(V_2 + m_2) + III(V_3 + m_3)] > [(D_2 - UA^E_{STP}) + (D_3 - UA^{III}_{STP})]$$

or

$$> II(C_2 + V_2 + m_2) + III(C_3 + V_3 + m_3)$$

The inequality reflects an excess of the surplus value (V + m) taking place in every division of the intellectual production over a cost of the intellectual services in IP Divisions II & III, without accounting for an unpaid portion of the assimilated resource STP ($UA^E_{STP}$, $UA^{III}_{STP}$).

In variant E of the reproduction schemes for the intellectual sphere the total sum of the produced intellectual services in Divisions II & III exceeds the volume of the material-intellectual values created in IP Division I.

**L. Variant** of a reproduction scheme of the intellectual sphere

$$\mathbf{D_1 > [D_2 + D_3]}$$
$$\mathbf{D_1 > [(D_2 - UA^E_{STP}) + (D_3 - UA^{III}_{STP})]}$$

This variant of the intellectual sphere reproduction has the situation when the sphere under consideration is in the making of a material and technical basis of «enlightenment», «education» and «entertainment» branches.

## Expanded Reproduction

### 1 condition

$$I(C_1 + V_1 + m_1) > (IC + IIC + IIIC)$$

or

$$I(V_1 + m_1) > (IIC + IIIC)$$

**2 condition:**

$$I(V_1 + m_1) + II(V_2 + m_2 + UA^E_{STP}) + III(V_3 + m_3 + UA^{III}_{STP}) > (D_2 + D_3)$$

where

$$D_2 = C_2 + V_2 + m_2 + UA^E_{STP}$$
$$D_3 = C_3 + V_3 + m_3 + UA^{III}_{STP}$$

unpaid portion of the assimilated resource STP.

At present not all the problems of reproduction are solved and we continue dealing with them.

## D. INTER-BRANCH BALANCE OF INTELLECTUALPRODUCTION

## GENERAL TERMS AND CONDITIONS FOR BALANCE IN THE INTELLECTUAL SPHERE

The structure of the intellectual «production» is first and foremost its branch structure:

### *Division 1: The branches producing intellectual values:*

- book production
- magazine production
- film production
- production of video radio-equipment.

### *Division 2: The branches producing intellectual services:*

- «Education»,
- «Enlightenment»:
  - «Culture»,
  - «Art»,
  - «Church»
- «Entertainment»:
  - «Sport-entertaining branch»,
  - «Film distribution»,
  - «TV Broadcasting»,
  - «Radio Broadcasting».

At a first approach one can see that the intellectual sphere represents an integral formation. This is a relatively autonomous field of a human application of labor. The intellectual sphere of production as an economic system is not only an aggregate of production processes of intellectual values (books, pictures, etc.) and of intellectual services—the services of a teacher, a musician, a dancer, etc., but also a distribution and consumption of these values and services, their exchange for other values and services, etc. These economic relations actually determine an economic structure of the intellectual sphere of production.

All the volume of an intellectual product is divided into the values and services of production consumption and into the values and services of non-production (personal) consumption.

a)  The Intellectual values created in Division I are distributed in four directions:

1.  The Intellectual values of a production purpose for Division I;

2.  The Intellectual values of a production purpose for Division II;

3.  The Intellectual values of a personal (non-production) purpose, which are consumed within Division I;

4.  The Intellectual values of a personal (non-production) purpose, which are consumed within Division II;


b)  The Intellectual services created in Intellectual sphere Division II are distributed in four directions:

1.  The Intellectual services of a production purpose, which are consumed within Intellectual sphere Division I;

2.  The Intellectual services of a production purpose, which are consumed within Intellectual sphere Division II;

3.  The Intellectual services of a non-production purpose, which are consumed within Intellectual sphere Division I;

4.  The Intellectual services of a non-production purpose, which are consumed within Intellectual sphere Division II.


From the beginning it is necessary to point out that every resource stream going out of the Intellectual sphere must find its reflection in the aggregate of indicators that allow us to evaluate its absolute and relative economic characteristics and criteria.

We use such characteristics as below:

$$h_1 = C_1/V_1; \quad DC_1/DV_1; \quad h_2 = C_2/V_2; \quad \Delta C_2/DV_2; \quad n_1 = m_1/V_1; \quad Dm_1/DV_1;$$
$$n_2 = (m_2 + A_{STP})/V_2; \quad (m_2 + A_{STP})/DV_2$$

And the following indicators as well:

$m_1$—surplus value of Intellectual production Division I.

$M_1 = m_1^a + m_1^c$

, where

$m_1^a$ —a portion of surplus value of Intellectual sphere Division I directed for accumulation («a» index);

$m_1^c$—a portion of surplus value of Intellectual sphere Division I directed for consumption («c» index);

$n_1$—a norm of accumulation in Intellectual sphere Division I $(m_1/V_1)$.

The above indicators can be written in another form, which is more convenient for calculations:

$m_1^a = n_1 \times m_1 = m_1/V_1 \times m_1$

$m_1^c = m_1 - m_1^a = m_1 - n_1 \times m_1 = (1 - n_1) \times m_1$

(m2 + ASTP)—a surplus value of Intellectual sphere Division II;

(m2 + ASTP)a—a portion of surplus value of Intellectual sphere Division II, which is directed for accumulation (services of an recreational character);

(m2 + ASTP)c—a portion of surplus value of Intellectual sphere Division II, which is directed for comsumption (services of an entertaining character);

(m2 + ASTP) = (m2 + ASTP)a + (m2 + ASTP)c

n2—a norm of accumulation in Intellectual sphere Division II ((m2 + ASTP)/V2);

(m2 + ASTP)a = n2 x (m2 + ASTP)

(m2 + ASTP)c = (m2 + ASTP) - n2 x (m2 + ASTP) = (m2 + ASTP) - n2 x m2 - n2 x ASTP =

= (1 - n2) x m2 + (1 - n2) x ASTP

## Calculation of $DV_1$

1) $\Delta V_1 = m_1{}^a - \Delta C_1$

2) $\Delta = m_1{}^a - \Delta V_1$

3) $\Delta C_1/\Delta V_1 = m_1{}^a/\Delta V_1 - \Delta V_1/\Delta V_1$

4) $h_1 = \Delta C_1/\Delta V_1 = m_1{}^a/\Delta V_1 - 1$

5) $m_1{}^a/\Delta V_1 = 1 + h_1$

6) $\Delta V_1 = \dfrac{1}{1+h_1} \times m_1{}^a = \dfrac{1}{1+h_1} \times n_1 \times m_1$

## Calculation of $\Delta C_1$

1) $m_1{}^a = \Delta C_1 + \Delta V_1$

2) $\Delta C_1 = m_1{}^a - \Delta V_1$

3) $\Delta C_1 = n_1 \times m_1 - \Delta V_1 = n_1 \times m_1 - \dfrac{1}{1+h_1} \times n_1 \times m_1$

4) $DC_1 \times (1 + h_1) = n_1 \times m_1 \times (1 + h_1) - n_1 \times m_1$

5) $\Delta C_1 = \dfrac{h \times h_1 \times m_1}{(1+h_1)} = \dfrac{h_1}{1+h_1} \times n_1 \times m_1$

## Calculation of $\Delta V_2$

1) $(m_2 + A_{STP})^a = \Delta V_2 + \Delta C_2$

2) $n_2 \times (m_2 + A_{STP}) = \Delta V_2 + \Delta C_2$

3) $\dfrac{n_2 \times (m_2 + A_{STP})}{\Delta V_2} = \dfrac{\Delta V_2}{\Delta V_2} + \dfrac{\Delta C_2}{\Delta V_2}$

4) $\dfrac{n_2 \times (m_2 + A_{STP})}{\Delta V_2} = 1 + h_2$

5) $\Delta V_2 = \dfrac{1}{1 + h_2} \times n_2 \times (m_2 + A_{STP})$

## Calculation of $\Delta C_2$

1) $(m_2 + A_{STP})^a = \Delta V_2 + \Delta C_2$

2) $n_2 \times (m_2 + A_{STP}) = \Delta V_2^{\,a} - \Delta V_2$

3) $\Delta C_2 = n_2 \times (m_2 + A_{STP}) - \Delta V_2$

4) $\Delta C_2 = n_2 \times (m_2 + A_{STP}) - \dfrac{1}{1 + h_2} \times n_2 \times (m_2 + A_{STP})$

5) $\Delta C_2 \times (1 + h_2) = (1 + h_2) \times h_2 \times (m_2 + A_{STP}) - h_2 \times (m_2 + A_{STP})$

6) $\Delta C_2 \times (1 + h_2) = (1 + h_2 - 1) \times h_2 \times (m_2 + A_{STP})$

7) $\Delta C_2 = \dfrac{h_2}{1 + h_2} \times h_2 \times (m_2 + A_{STP})$

# IMPLEMENTATION SCHEME
# OF THE INTELLECTUAL PRODUCT

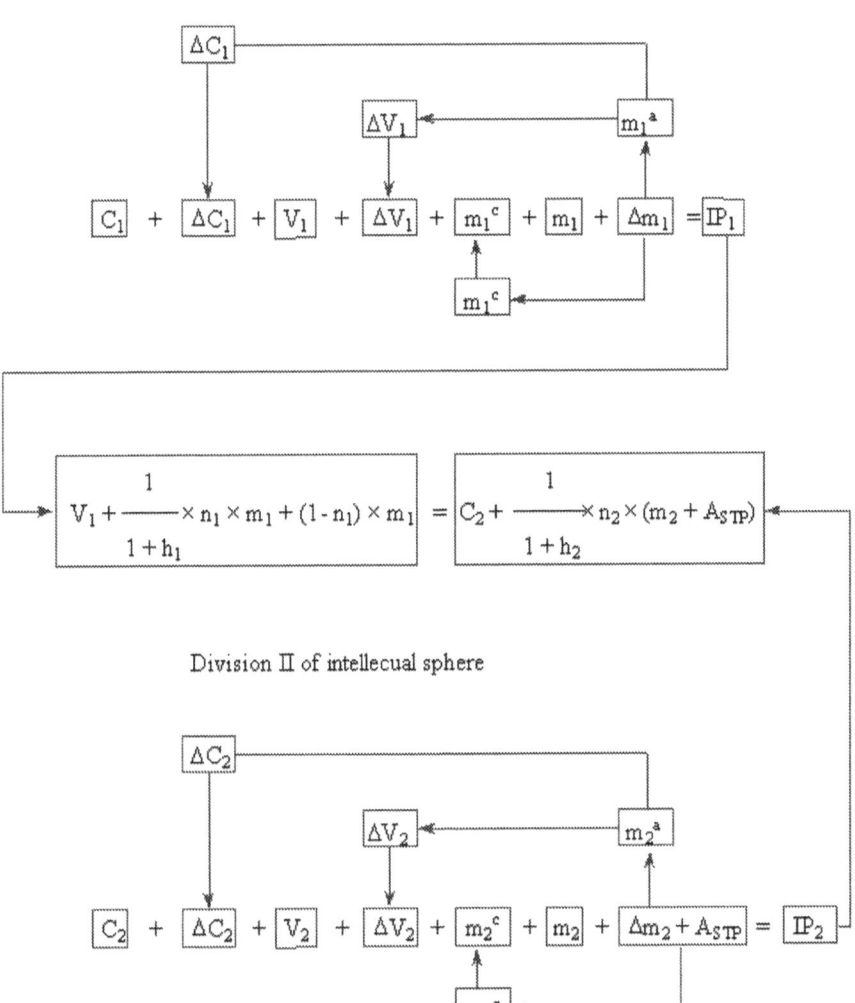

## TERMS AND CONDITIONS FOR BALANCED EXCHANGE IN THE INTELLECTUAL SPHERE

A balanced exchange between Intellectual sphere Division I and Division II is only possible provided there takes place an unimpeded exchange of Intellectual values for Intellectual services.

***Condition 1***. If the Intellectual services do not include an economically estimated assimilated resource of spare time of population ($A_{STP}$), it is necessary to produce more services at the value of $A_{STP}$ to compensate the disparity (of an unequivalent exchange) in Intellectual sphere Division II. A continuous exchange takes place in this case.

***Condition 2***. A balanced exchange of all the components of Intellectual values ($C_1 + V_1 + m_1$) and all the components of Intellectual services ($C_2 + V_2 + m_2 + A_{STP}$) requires a definite condition. Within its boundaries, Intellectual sphere Division I advances (defines) its needs in the Intellectual services to the amount equal to the needs of Intellectual sphere Division II in the Intellectual values.

***Condition 3***. A surplus value in Intellectual sphere Division I must exceed past labor expenses in Division II

$$(IV_1 + Im_1) > IIC_2$$

***Condition 4***. In terms and conditions of the expanding Intellectual sphere, the volume of increments in a surplus value ($V_2$ and $DV_2$) and a portion of the incomes (which are directed for consumption ($m_1^c$) must be equal to the volume of means, which are required to restore the past labor expenses plus delta of the past labor expenses (caused by the production enlargement):

$$V_1 + \Delta V_1 + m_1{}^c = \Delta_2 + \Delta C_2$$

When calculating $C_2$, $DV_2$, it is necessary to use a surplus product of Division II accounting for an assimilated resource of spare time of population ($m_2 + A_{STP}$). Moreover, it is necessary to bear in mind that an assimilation of this specific resource by Intellectual services is executed on two levels: educational and recreation. In this sense $A_{STP}$, which is assimilated with an educational purpose, is to be considered as a portion of the Intellectual services used in an accumulation mode. Another portion of $A_{STP}$ of an recreation character is directed for consumption only.

If we substitute the developed indicators in this equality with account for the spare time resource of population assimilated by Intellectual services, we obtain as below:

$$V_1 + \frac{1}{1 + h_1} \times n_1 \times m_1 + (1 - n_1) \times m_1 = C_2 + \frac{1}{1 + h_2} \times n_2 \times (m_2 + A_{STP})$$

The equality reflects the fact that supply of Intellectual values equals to demand in Intellectual services with account for assimilated resource STP.

**_Condition 5._** A norm of accumulation in Intellectual sphere Division II ($n_2$) must be calculated as per the formula $(m_2 + A_{STP})/V_2$. Otherwise, it would be underestimated by the amount of the spare time resource assimilated with the Intellectual services. It would finally lead to an increase in the accumulation norm of Division I.

Execution of the above conditions makes it possible to avoid imbalance in exchange relations in Intellectual sphere.

The author of the present book considers an intellectual sphere as an economic system that consists of three Divisions:

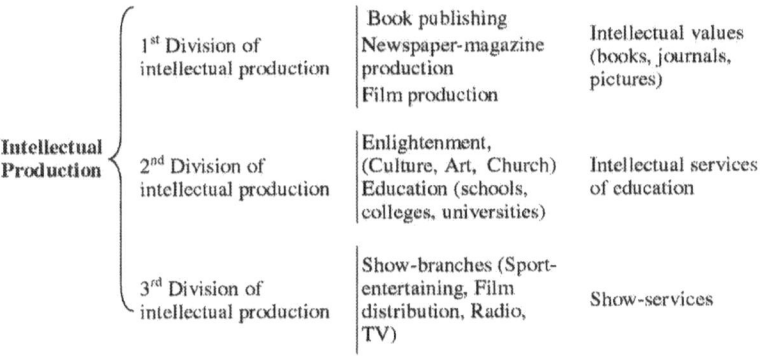

| Intellectual Production | 1st Division of intellectual production | Book publishing<br>Newspaper-magazine production<br>Film production | Intellectual values (books, journals, pictures) |
|---|---|---|---|
| | 2nd Division of intellectual production | Enlightenment, (Culture, Art, Church) Education (schools, colleges, universities) | Intellectual services of education |
| | 3rd Division of intellectual production | Show-branches (Sport-entertaining, Film distribution, Radio, TV) | Show-services |

Thus, for instance, *«the developed countries have created strong, monopolized publishing, radio- and TV- conglomerations, newspaper trusts which have their affiliates in different countries. As a rule, they are owned by international monopolies. A bank's financial capital splices with intellectual production, a «financial and cultural» oligarchy is created».*

*«The film studios deal with film production—this is a sphere of production of cultural values. After a film is created, it goes to the film distribution organizations, but first it is being duplicated at special film industry factories. The work on duplication and copy making also enters the sphere of production. The activities of the film distribution organizations, film making institutions, cinemas and theatres, lie within a sphere of cultural servicing. It is with their help that the services are created, as these institutions directly deal with servicing and meeting intellectual demands and needs, they organize and maintain a transfer process of cultural values from their creators to their consumers».*

## A. INTER-BRANCH BALANCE OF INTELLECTUAL    PRODUCTION DIVISION 1

For the last 30 years in intellectual production Division № I there has been a rapid equipping   with updated machines and corresponding technologies for the production of intellectual values (books, pictures, films, icons).[25] In other words, a surplus product[26] is being created in Intellectual Production Division I, the same as in any other branch of material production. A Product of labor of Intellectual Production Division I may be put down as follows:

$$C_1^I + V_1^I + M_1^I = m_1^I$$

, where

25  *«Abroad», №51. «Shpringer's Empire is the largest in Europe weekly magazine «Her Ztu» (a circulation of 3.3 million), the largest at the Continent newspaper «Billed» (a circulation of 5.3 million ), regional newspapers «Hamburger Abendblat», «Berlin Morgen Post» and «Bc Zed», magazines of Radio- and TV-programmes «Fuek Ur», «Bildvokhe», women's magazines «Billed der Frau» and «Journale», Sunday publication «Velt Am Zontag» and «Billed Am Zontag», special magazines, novel-newspapers and books. The Concern's turnover comes to 24 Billion Marks».*

26  *«A capitalisation of the intellectual value production, its serving to private selfish aims, a development of a competitive struggle in the production sphere of an intellectual culture and art - these are the basic features characteristic of a production of the intellectual values in terms of today's capitalism».* (Orlov V.N., «Culture and leisure», pages 16-17).

$C'_I$—means and instruments of labor consumed while creating intellectual values;

$V^I_I + M^I_I$—required and surplus labor to produce intellectual values.

The above formula allows us to draw Block № 1 of Intellectual Production inter-branch balance.

Let $P_1$, $P_2$, ... $P_n$ be results of labor of the branches forming intellectual production division № 1 interconnection of these branches (polygraph, publications, etc.) is written down as a system of linear equations:

$$\begin{cases} a_{11}P_1 + a_{12}P_2 + a_{13}P_3 + ... + a_{1n}P_n + VD_1 = P_1 \\ a_{21}P_1 + a_{22}P_2 + a_{23}P_3 + ... + a_{2n}P_n + VD_2 = P_2 \\ ...\ \ ...\ \ ...\ \ ...\ \ ...\ \ ...\ \ ...\ \ ...\ \ ...\ \ ... \\ a_{n1}P_1 + a_{n2}P_2 + a_{n3}P_3 + ... + a_{nn}P_n + VD_n = P_n \end{cases}$$

$$(1)$$

, where

$a_{IJ}$ —coefficients of material expenses in i- branches of intellectual production division №1 tied up with the creation of j- means of labor and instruments of labor of intellectual production;

$Vd_I$ —Net Income of i- branch of intellectual production division № 1, without a cost of material expenses;

n —number of branches of the division.

From the above system of equations it follows that GDP of intellectual production division N 1 comes to be as below:

$$\sum_{i=1}^{n} P_i = \sum_{i=1}^{n} V d_i + \sum_{i=1}^{n} \sum_{j=1}^{n} a_{ij} P_i$$

$$i = 1...n, \quad j = 1...n.$$

$$(1a)^{27}$$

Ratio of expenses of this block $a_{ij}$ reflects an amount of depreciation (consumption of fixed capital) $A_{ij}$ and expenses of direct labor $T_{ij}$-, i.e.

$$a_{ij} = A_{ij} + T_{ij} \quad a = C + V$$

Based upon the above, the 1st Block of inter-branch balance of the intellectual production would be as follows:

$$\begin{cases} P_1 - (a_{11}P_1 + a_{12}P_2 + a_{13}P_3 + \cdots + a_{1n}P_n) = VD_1 \\ P_2 - (a_{21}P_1 + a_{22}P_2 + a_{23}P_3 + \cdots + a_{2n}P_n) = VD_2 \\ \cdots \; \cdots \; \cdots \; \cdots \; \cdots \; \cdots \; \cdots \; \cdots \; \cdots \; \cdots \; \cdots \\ P_n - (a_{n1}P_1 + a_{n2}P_2 + a_{n3}P_3 + \cdots + a_{nn}P_n) = VD_n \end{cases}$$

$$(1b)$$

and a matrix of ratios would be as follows:

$$A = \begin{pmatrix} (1-a_{11}), & -a_{12}, & -a_{13}, & \cdots & a_{1n}, \\ -a_{21}, & (1-a_{22}), & -a_{23}, & \cdots & a_{2n}, \\ \cdots & \cdots & \cdots & \cdots & \cdots \\ -a_{n1}, & -a_{n2}, & -a_{n3}, & \cdots & (1-a_{nn}) \end{pmatrix} \quad (6.1c)$$

On the basis of (1a), (1b) and (1c) the inter-branch balance of intellectual production would be as follows in matrix form:

---

27    *I variant* $C^I + V^I + A^E_{STP} = P^I$

*II variant* $C^{II} + V^{II} + m^{II} + A^E_{STP} = P^I_{II}$

$$Ap + Vd = P$$

The expression (1b) constitutes a system of linear equations. Its solution is usually carried out with widely known methods. For instance, with the method of Gauss or Jordan-Gauss. A general solution that allows to determine all the values of $P_1$ might look as follows if one is guided with a Kramer's Rule:

$$P_1 = \frac{D_1}{D}; \quad P_2 = \frac{D_2}{D}; \quad \cdots \quad P_n = \frac{D_k}{D}$$

(2a)

, where

$$D = \begin{vmatrix} (1-a_{11}), & -a_{12}, & -a_{13}, & \cdots & a_{1n}, \\ -a_{21}, & (1-a_{22}), & -a_{23}, & \cdots & a_{2n}, \\ \cdots & \cdots & \cdots & \cdots & \cdots \\ -a_{n1}, & -a_{n2}, & -a_{n3}, & \cdots & (1-a_{nn}) \end{vmatrix}$$ (6.2b)

D—a determinant of a system of equations (2b), and the condition for its solution is:

$$D = 0 \qquad (2c)$$

Determinants $D_K$ (k = 1, 2, ...n) come out of the determinants of a system (1b) by a change of k- column (i.e. a ratio column for the being determined $P_1$) with the columns of spare members.

$$D_k = \begin{vmatrix} (1-a_{11}), -a_{12}, \ldots, -a_{1k-1}, Vd_1, -a_{1k+1}, \ldots, a_{1n} \\ -a_{2,12}, (1-a_{22}), \ldots, -a_{2,k-1}, Vd_2, -a_{2,k+1}, \ldots, a_{2n} \\ \cdots\cdots\cdots\cdots\cdots\cdots\cdots\cdots\cdots\cdots\cdots \\ -a_{n1}, -a_{n2}, \ldots, -a_{n,k-1}, Vd_n, -a_{n,k+1}, \ldots, (1-a_{nn}) \end{vmatrix}$$

(2d)

As an example we can consider a system accounting for the interaction of the three leading branches of the 1st division: book publishing, periodicals, film production (they are related to the relevant indices – «T», «T», «II». As a general, in accordance with (1b), the system is as follows:

$$\begin{cases} P_T(1-a_{TT}) + P_K(-a_{TK}) + P_\Pi(-a_{T\Pi}) = Vd_T \\ P_T(-a_{KT)} + P_K(1-a_{KK}) + P_\Pi(-a_{K\Pi}) = Vd_K \\ P_T(-a_{\Pi T}) + P_K(-a_{PK}) + P_K(1-a_{\Pi\Pi}) = Vd_n \end{cases}$$

In this case a determinant of the system would be expressed as follows (2b):

$$D = \begin{vmatrix} (1-a_{TT}), (-a_{TK}), (-a_{T\Pi}) \\ (-a_{KT}), (1-a_{KK}), (-a_{K\Pi}) \\ (-a_{\Pi T}), (-a_{\Pi K}), (1-a_{\Pi\Pi}) \end{vmatrix} \neq 0$$

A solution is found according to (2a)

$$P_T = \frac{D_T}{D}; \quad P_K = \frac{D_K}{D}; \quad P_\Pi = \frac{D_\Pi}{D}$$

Where, in accordance with (2)

$$D_T = \begin{vmatrix} Vd_T, (-a_{TK}), (-a_{T\Pi}) \\ Vd_K, (-a_{KK}), (-a_{K\Pi}) \\ Vd_\Pi, (-a_{\Pi K}), (1-a_{\Pi\Pi}) \end{vmatrix}$$

$$D_K = \begin{vmatrix} (1-a_{TT}), Vd_T, (-a_{T\Pi}) \\ (-a_{KT}), Vd_K, (-a_{K\Pi}) \\ (-a_{\Pi T}), Vd_\Pi, (1-a_{\Pi\Pi}) \end{vmatrix}$$

$$D_\Pi = \begin{vmatrix} (1-a_{TT}), Vd_T, (-a_{T\Pi}) \\ (-a_{KT}), Vd_K, (-a_{K\Pi}) \\ (-a_{\Pi T}), Vd_\Pi, (1-a_{\Pi\Pi}) \end{vmatrix}$$

Represented in a compact form, the system of equations of intellectual production division № 1 has a solution with unknown meanings of production of intellectual values, at the preset vector of a final product stream

$$P = (I - A)^{-1} Vd \quad (2)$$

, where

(I-A)$^{-1}$    —a matrix of coefficients of full expenses in intellectual production division № 1;

P    —a stream of labor results of all the branches division № 1—a vector oriented in the space of n-branches;

Vd    —a stream of net income being produced in division № 1.

## B.  INTER-BRANCH BALANCE OF INTELLECTUAL PRODUCTION DIVISION 2

I include only the sub-branches producing intellectual services—«Enlightenment», «Education» into the 2$^{nd}$ Division of the intellectual sphere. Product of labor of Intellectual Production Division 2 may be put down as follows:

$$C^I_{II} + V^I_{II} + A^E_{STP} = P^I_{II} \quad (3)$$

, whereat

$C^I_{II}$    —means of labor, instruments of labor—technical means consumed while producing «Enlightenment», «Education» services;

$V^I_{II}$    —wages of «Enlightenment», «Education» employees;

$A^E_{STP}$    —a paid population spare time resource (STP) assimilated by institutions of «Enlightenment», «Education».

In other words, «Enlightenment», «Education» services are divided into wages and a paid resource STP assimilated by the educational institutions.

Intellectual production division № 2 has a definite number of branches $n$, a product of labor of each can be written as $d_1, d_2, d_3, \ldots d_n$. Interconnection between intellectual sphere branches can be expressed with the following system of linear equations:

$$\begin{cases} c_{11}d_1 + c_{12}d_2 + c_{13}d_3 + \ldots + c_{1n}d_n + A^E_{STP1} = d_1 \\ c_{21}d_1 + c_{22}d_2 + c_{23}d_3 + \ldots + c_{2n}d_n + A^E_{STP2} = d_2 \\ \ldots\ldots\ldots\ldots\ldots\ldots\ldots\ldots\ldots\ldots\ldots\ldots \\ c_{n1}d_1 + c_{n2}d_2 + c_{n3}d_3 + \ldots + c_{nn}d_n + A^E_{STPn} = d_n \end{cases} \quad \text{(3a)}_{28}$$

, where

$c_{ij}$ —ratios of material expenses in i- branches of intellectual production division № 2, tied up with the creation of j- services of «Enlightenment», «Education»;

$A^E_{STP}$—an assimilated resource of population spare time (STP) of «Enlightenment», «Education» branches.

From this system of equations it follows that the product of intellectual production division № 2 would be solid as below:

$$\sum_{i=1}^{n} d_i = \sum_{i=1}^{n}\sum_{j=1}^{n} c_{ij}d_{ij} + \sum_{i=1}^{n} A^E_{STPi}$$

$$i = 1\ldots n, \quad j = 1\ldots n. \tag{3b}$$

Peculiarity of the 2nd block of inter-branch balance of intellectual production is that ratios $c_{ij}$ reflect a volume of depreciation ($AA_{ij}$) and expenses of direct labor ($TT_{ij}$) in i- branch of the intellectual production which are aimed to produce j—services of «Enlightenment», «Education»:

$$c_{ij} = AA_{ij} + TT_{ij}$$

---

28    I variant $C^I_{II} + V^I_{II} + A^E_{STP} = P^I_{II}$
        II variant $C^I_{II} + V^I_{II} + m_{II} + A^E_{STP} = P^I_{II}$

On the basis of the above system of linear equations of intellectual production division 2 may be written as follows:

$$\begin{cases} d_1 - (c_{11}d_1 + c_{12}d_2 + c_{13}d_3 + \dots + c_{1n}d_n) = A^E_{STP1} \\ d_2 - (c_{21}d_1 + c_{22}d_2 + c_{23}d_3 + \dots + c_{2n}d_n) = A^E_{STP2} \\ \dots \quad \dots \quad \dots \quad \dots \quad \dots \quad \dots \quad \dots \quad \dots \quad \dots \quad \dots \quad \dots \\ d_n - (c_{n1}d_1 + c_{n2}d_2 + c_{n3}d_3 + \dots + c_{nn}d_n) = A^E_{STPn} \end{cases}$$

(3c)

and a matrix of ratios would appear as follows:

$$AA = \begin{pmatrix} (1-c_{11}), & -c_{12}, & -c_{13}, & \dots & c_{1n}, \\ -c_{21}, & (1-c_{22}), & -c_{23}, & \dots & c_{2n}, \\ \dots & \dots & \dots & \dots & \dots \\ -c_{n1}, & -c_{n2}, & -c_{n3}, & \dots & (1-c_{nn}) \end{pmatrix}$$

(3d)

The system of linear equations is completely analogous to the system (1b) considered before, and consequently it can also be solved with known methods.

A determinant for a matrix of equation ratios (3c) would be

$$D = \begin{vmatrix} (1-c_{11}), -c_{12}, -c_{13}, \dots, -c_{1n} \\ -c_{21}, (1-c_{22}), -c_{23}, \dots, -c_{2n} \\ \dots\dots\dots\dots\dots\dots\dots\dots\dots\dots\dots \\ -c_{n1}, -c_{n2}, -c_{n3}, \dots, (1-c_{nn}) \end{vmatrix}$$

and the solutions could be presented as

$$d_1 = \frac{D_1}{D}; \quad d_2 = \frac{D_2}{D}; \quad \dots \quad d_n = \frac{D_K}{D},$$

where $D_K$ are determined in accordance with (2)

$$D_K = \begin{vmatrix} (1-c_{11}),-c_{12},...,-c_{1,k-1}, A_{STP1},-c_{1,k+1},...,-a_{1n} \\ -c_{21},(1-c_{22}),...,-c_{2,k-1}, A_{STP2},-c_{2,k+1},...,-a_{2n} \\ ........................................................... \\ -a_{n1},-c_{n2},...,-c_{n,k-1}, A_{STPn},-c_{n,k+1},...,c_{nn} \end{vmatrix}$$

The system of linear equations can be taken as an example for two leading branches of division № 2, for «Enlightenment» and «Education», inserting indices «П» and «О» respectively.

$$\begin{cases} d_n - (c_{nn}d_n + c_{nM}d_M) = A_{STP1} \\ d_O - (c_{Mn}d_n + c_{MM}d_O) = A_{STP2} \end{cases}$$

The following expression would be a determinant of the system

$$D = \begin{vmatrix} 1-c_{\Pi\Pi},-c_{\Pi O} \\ -c_{O\Pi},1-c_{OO} \end{vmatrix} \neq 0$$

Values $d_\Pi$, $d_O$ can be found out of the expressions

$$d_\Pi = \frac{D_\Pi}{D}; \quad d_K = \frac{D_K}{D};$$

$$D_n = \begin{vmatrix} A_{STP1},-c_{no} \\ A_{STP2},1-c_{no} \end{vmatrix}$$

$$D_K = \begin{vmatrix} 1-c_{nn}, A_{STP1} \\ -c_{on}, A_{STP2} \end{vmatrix}$$

On the basis of the above, a system of equations of intellectual production inter-branch balance would have a matrix type as follows:

$$AAd + A_S = d$$

This system of equations of intellectual production has a solution with the unknown values of the production volumes of «Enlightenment», «Education» services, with the preset vector of a final product:

$$d = (I - A)^{-1} A_S,$$

, where

$(I - A)^{-1}$- a matrix constituting a system of total expenses in producing the services of «Enlightenment» and «Education».

## C. INTER-BRANCH BALANCE OF INTELLECTUAL PRODUCTION DIVISION 3

Aiming to eliminate errors that may appear as a result of mixing intellectual branches: «Enlightenment», «Education» and «Entertainment» branches, I propose that «show-branches» are to be singled out into intellectual production division № 3.

$$C^I_{III} + V^I_{III} + A^S_{STP2} = P^I_{III} \ (4)^{29}$$

, where

—means of labor, instruments of labor—technical means of «Entertainment» services' production consumed at a process of creation of the latter;

$V^I_{III}$, $m^I_{III}$—a wage and surplus product in the «Entertainment» branch;

$A^S_{STP2}$ —a resource of spare time population (STP) assimilated by «Entertainment» branch;

$P^I_{III}$ —intellectual services of labor division 3.

Division 3 of the intellectual production has a definite number of «Entertainment» branch $n$, a product of labor of each of them can be written as $d_1, d_2, d_3, ... d_n$. An interconnection of the intellectual sphere branches can be expressed with the following system of linear equations:

---

29   $I \ variant \ C^I_{III} + V^I_{III} + A^S_{STP} = P^I_{III}$

$II \ variant \ C^I_{III} + V^I_{III} + m^I_{III} + A^S_{STP} = P^I_{III}$

$$
\begin{cases}
c_{11}d_1 + c_{12}d_2 + c_{13}d_3 + K + c_{1n}d_n + VDD_1 = d_1 \\
c_{21}d_1 + c_{22}d_{21} + c_{23}d_3 + K + c_{2n}d_n + VDD_2 = d_2 \\
\text{...  ...  ...  ...  ...  ...  ...  ...  ...  ...  ...} \\
c_{n1}d_1 + c_{n2}d_2 + c_{n3}d_3 + K + c_{nn}d_n + VDD_n = d_n
\end{cases}
$$

$$(4a)$$

, where

$c_{IJ}$ —ratios of material expenses in i- branches of intellectual production division 3 tied up with the creation of j-«Entertainment»-services;

$VDD_I$—a Net Income of i- branch of intellectual production division 3.

Out of this system of equations it follows that the product of intellectual production division 3 is written down as below:

$$
\sum_{i=1}^{n} d_i = \sum_{i=1}^{n} VDD_i + \sum_{i=1}^{n}\sum_{j=1}^{n} c_{ij}d_{ij}
$$

$$
i = 1...n, \quad j = 1...n. \tag{4b}
$$

A peculiarity of the 3rd block of interbranch balance of the intellectual production is that ratios with ij reflect a volume of depreciation ($AA_{ij}$) and expenses of the direct labor ($TT_{ij}$) in i-branch of the intellectual production spent for the production of j- show-services:

$$
c_{IJ} = AA_{IJ} + TT_{IJ}
$$

On the basis of the above a system of linear equations of intellectual production division № 3 is possible to be written as follows:

$$\begin{cases} d_1 - (c_{11}d_1 + c_{12}d_2 + c_{13}d_3 + \dots + c_{1n}d_n) = A^s_{STP1} \\ d_2 - (c_{21}d_1 + c_{22}d_2 + c_{23}d_3 + \dots + c_{2n}d_n) = A^s_{STP2} \\ \dots \ \dots \ \dots \ \dots \ \dots \ \dots \ \dots \ \dots \ \dots \ \dots \ \dots \\ d_n - (c_{n1}d_1 + c_{n2}d_2 + c_{n3}d_3 + \dots + c_{nn}d_n) = A^s_{STPn} \end{cases}$$

(4c)

and a matrix of ratios would appear as follows:

$$AA = \begin{pmatrix} (1-c_{11}), & -c_{12}, & -c_{13}, & \dots & c_{1n}, \\ -c_{21}, & (1-c_{22}), & -c_{23}, & \dots & c_{2n}, \\ \dots & \dots & \dots & \dots & \dots \\ -c_{n1}, & -c_{n2}, & -c_{n3}, & \dots & (1-c_{nn}) \end{pmatrix}$$

(4d)

The system of linear equations is completely analogous to the system (1.b) considered before, and consequently it can also be solved with known methods.

A determinant for a matrix of equation ratios (6) would be based upon the above, the system of linear equations of intellectual production division 3 is possible to be written down as follows:

$$AA{\cdot}d + VDD = d$$

This system of equations of the intellectual production has its solution with the unknown values of these «Entertainment» services production volumes, with the vector of a final product

$$d = (I - A)^{-1} VDD$$

, whereat

$(I - A)^{-1}$—a matrix-system of ratios of complete expenses spent to produce the «Entertainment» services.

The inter-branch balance of the intellectual sphere of production proposed hereby corresponds to the real facts taking place in our every day life.

# ATTACHMENT

## NEW BOOK: THE INTELLECTUAL SPHERE—STOCKS EXCHANGE INDICES

Synopsis

At present in European countries the following indices are used:

FTSE, CAC-40, HEX-25, ASE-20, BEL-20, OBX, KFX, AEX, MIBTEL, SMI, XETRA, DAX.

Using these indices we encounter a situation when, being aware of the stock exchange activity on the one part of the market, we are ignorant of the trends on the other: the market of intellectual services, Internet services, transport services and medical care services.

I imply those sectors of the market where economists have not elaborated a system of economic estimates, criteria, indicators of the stock exchange activity.

Introduction

Statistic analysis shows that for the last 100 years the services part of GDP in the developed countries has increased up to 70%. In this connection the ratio of the stock market securities should be:

- stock of enterprises creating material values—30%

- stock of companies creating services—70%

This is an optimum ratio or else we may have distortions in estimating general situation with securities.

It is necessary to point out that securities have to be systematized according to the sphere they belong to. In this situation we should carry out a functional classification of stocks.

The situation in the system of estimates will essentially improve if we have specific stock exchange indices for every sphere of economy. In that case it would be easier to analyze business activity and define which sector of economy is lagging behind in tempo of development and which one is moving ahead of the average rate.

I suggest the following abbreviations for the indices of the stock market activity be introduced:

- GOVERNMENT Sphere—Stock Exchange Index – securities of the sphere of state power;

- Mass Media Sphere—Stock exchange Index for 1000 companies of the intellectual sphere;

- Intellectual Sphere—Stock Exchange Index for 1000 companies of the intellectual sphere;

- Internet Sphere—Stock Exchange Index for 1000 companies of the Internet sphere;

- Medical Sphere—Stock Exchange Index for 1000 companies of the medical sphere;

- TRS Sphere—Stock Exchange Index for 1000 companies of the transport sphere;

- MIL Sphere—Stock Exchange Index for 1000 companies of the military sphere.

It will be necessary to work out a relevant economic theory for each of these indices to avoid logical mistakes.

It is necessary to point out that there is an obvious connection between the cost estimate of stock and the cost estimate of the results of company activities as shown below:

1.

| Economic theory: Cost estimate of the activity results of the intellectual sphere enterprises | ←→ | Cost estimate of the stocks of the intellectual sphere enterprises | ←→ | Index of the stock market activity of the intellectual sphere |
|---|---|---|---|---|

2.

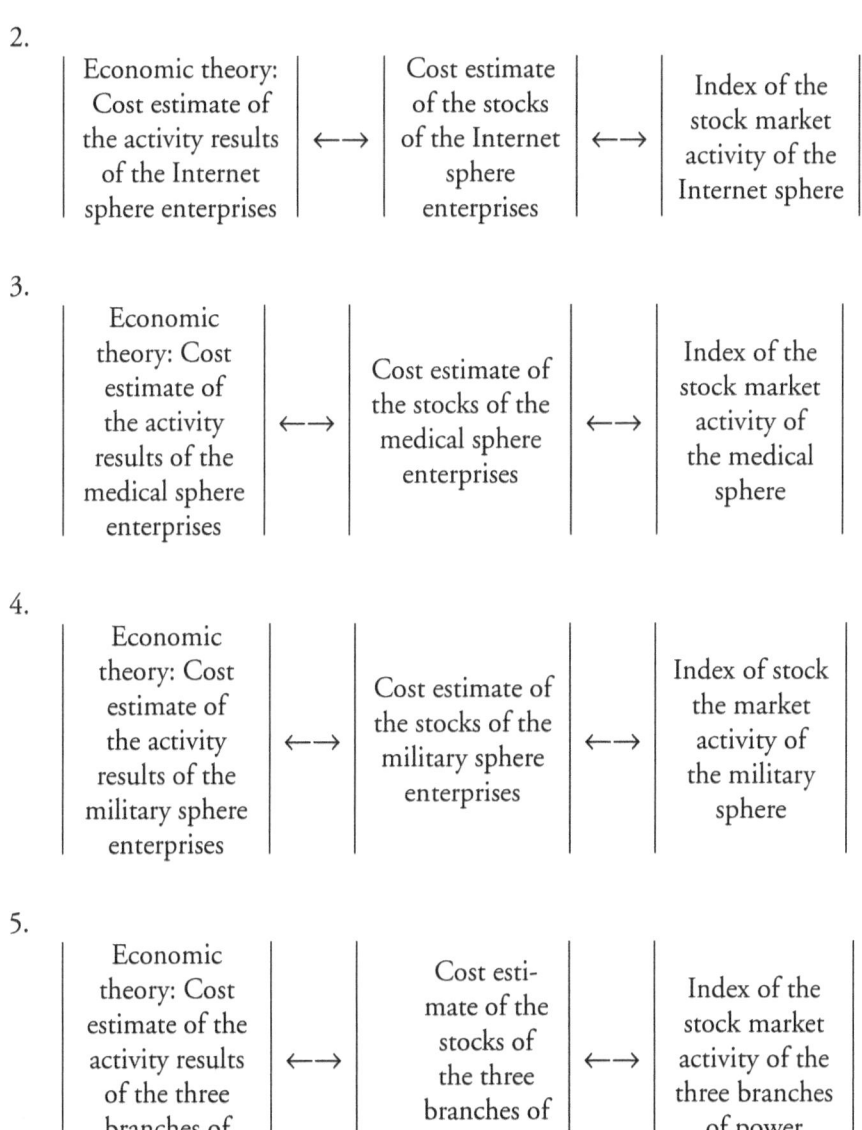

| Economic theory: Cost estimate of the activity results of the Internet sphere enterprises | ←→ | Cost estimate of the stocks of the Internet sphere enterprises | ←→ | Index of the stock market activity of the Internet sphere |

3.

| Economic theory: Cost estimate of the activity results of the medical sphere enterprises | ←→ | Cost estimate of the stocks of the medical sphere enterprises | ←→ | Index of the stock market activity of the medical sphere |

4.

| Economic theory: Cost estimate of the activity results of the military sphere enterprises | ←→ | Cost estimate of the stocks of the military sphere enterprises | ←→ | Index of stock the market activity of the military sphere |

5.

| Economic theory: Cost estimate of the activity results of the three branches of power | ←→ | Cost estimate of the stocks of the three branches of power | ←→ | Index of the stock market activity of the three branches of power |

This is an optimum ratio or else we may have distortions in estimating general situation with securities.

It is necessary to point out that securities have to be systematized according to the sphere they belong to. In this situation we should carry out a functional classification of stocks.

We can judge of the general situation in macroeconomy provided we possess a ramified system of estimates, criteria, indicators to be able to establish the starting points of the downfalls or growth in each of the spheres: material, intellectual, Internet, transport, medical care, military, sphere of power.

The situation in the system of estimates will essentially improve if we have specific stock exchange indices for every sphere of economy. In that case it would be easier to analyze business activity and define which sector of economy is lagging behind in tempo of development and which one is moving ahead of the average rate.

It is necessary to point out that there is an obvious connection between the cost estimate of stock and the cost estimate of the results of company activities as shown below:

1.

| Economic theory: Cost estimate of the activity results of the intellectual sphere enterprises | ⟷ | Cost estimate of the stocks of the intellectual s0phere enterprises | ⟷ | Index of the stock market activity of the intellectual sphere |

2.

| Economic theory: Cost estimate of the activity results of the Internet sphere enterprises | ⟷ | Cost estimate of the stocks of the internet sphere enterprises | ⟷ | Index of the stock market activity of the Internet sphere |

3.

| Economic theory: Cost estimate of the activity results of the medical sphere enterprises | ⟷ | Cost estimate of the stocks of the medical sphere enterprises | ⟷ | Index of the stock market activity of the medical sphere |

4.

| Economic theory: Cost estimate of the activity results of the military sphere enterprises | ⟷ | Cost estimate of the stocks of the military sphere enterprises | ⟷ | Index of the stock market activity of the military sphere |

5.

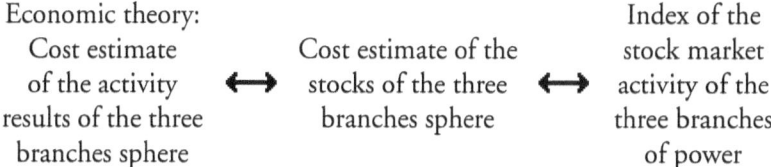

I suggest the following abbreviations for the indices of the stock market activity be introduced:

- Intellectual Sphere-Stock Exchange Index for 100 or 200 companies of the intellectual sphere;

- Internet Sphere-Stock Exchange Index for 100 (200) companies of the Internet sphere;

- Medical Sphere-Stock Exchange Index for 100 or 200 companies of the medical sphere;

- TRS Sphere-Stock Exchange Index for 100 or 200 companies of the transport sphere;

- MIL Sphere-Stock Exchange Index for 100 or 200 companies of the military sphere;

- GOV Sphere-Stock Exchange Index – securities of the sphere of state power.

It will be necessary to work out a relevant economic theory for each of these indices to avoid logical mistakes.

## A. THE STOCK EXCHANGE INDEX FOR THE INTELLECTUAL SPHERE

Now it is possible to assess the state of the security markets of the intellectual sphere with reference to those companies alone that produce intellectual values in material form: books, newspapers, magazines, films etc.

However, for the companies producing intellectual services, evaluation of security markets will be more difficult. The main problem here consists in the absence of a logically grounded linkage between the cost of stock and the cost estimate of intellectual services.

## FIRST VARIANT OF ESTIMATES

Cost estimate of the stocks of the intellectual sphere enterprises  Cost estimate of the activity results of the intellectual sphere enterprises without taking into account the resource of the spare time of the population (ASTP) assimilated by intellectual services

## SECOND VARIANT OF ESTIMATES

Cost estimate of the stocks of the intellectual sphere enterprises  Cost estimate of the activity results of the intellectual sphere enterprises including the resource of the spare time of the population (ASTP) assimilated by intellectual services

In these assessments as the reader can see, we shall take into account not only traditional but also untraditional resources in the form of assimilated spare time of the population resource ($A_{STP}$). The inclusion of them allows us to revise the concept of the stock values of the intellectual sphere enterprises. Such estimates are used while taking decisions on the expediency of investments in stocks.

**From the author**

While considering the economic problems of the intellectual sphere, the first thing we should do is to draw a line of watershed between past and present ideas in the theory.

This should be done because if we adhere to the old dogmas on this theme, left to us by our forefathers, we shall each time, in each direction of research «step on a rake». These dogmas are scattered everywhere—both here and there. Whenever we make a step forward a «big-wig» from Karl Marks, David Rikardo arises at once.

We should avoid such a thorny progress on the bushes of the economic theory. That is why it is necessary to create a new system of economic dogmas of the third millennium that are distinct from those, which have existed for more than 200 years, in the theory of the intellectual sphere.

Thus, it is necessary to admit that:

1. «A dancer», «a musician», «a clergyman» are productive workers of society;

2. The specific character of their work, acting as service, is also an economic product;

3.  The branches of intellectual sphere form their own specific part of GDP, NDP, NI;

4.  Intellectual values and services are created in economic space (and not in the outer space);

5.  The human resource during its spare time is a bearer of economic relations;

6.  Economic estimations can be of conventional and unconventional nature.

7.  We should not limit the research of the intellectual sphere with the frames of real numbers.

Here we should use real, imaginary and complex numbers.

If we unite the above-mentioned statements we will receive the heptahedron that determines the area of our theoretical interests. The area where there is no place for old dogmas.

The structure of the Intellectual sphere in each country has its peculiarity. Its parameters depend on many factors:

- financial resources of the country;

- purchasing power of the population;

- attitude of a state towards the spare time of the population;

- cost estimation of the spare time of the population;

- quality of a material base of the intellectual sphere;

- professional readiness of staff of intellectual sphere etc.

Integration of the European countries into a unified economic system (EU) suggests a close interconnection of such branches as Education, Culture, Art, the Church, Film circulation, TV, Radio and Sport-Entertainments in the framework of the European Union.

Here we have to deal with economic estimations to establish the ongoing integrational process in the Intellectual sphere within the EU. Moreover we shall not be content with one or two, but deal with a system of assessments.

No significant effort has been made for the last hundred years to elaborate the theory of the intellectual sphere. It has not been developed in spite of the fact that this sector of economy has been rapidly expanding owing to the expansion of the Education, Enlightenment and Entertainment branches. However, this trend has remained unnoticed on the part of the specialists in the economic theory.

At present, the integrational processes in the intellectual sphere within EU can be assessed only at the expenditure level, i.e. expenses of the education, enlightenment and entertainment branches. Although a simple addition of the Intellectual sphere expenditures may prove more than commonplace. The resultant component of the EU intellectual sphere involves certain problems, in particular:

Problem I. While estimating the economic results of the intellectual sphere such indicators as the «quantity of visitors», the «quantity of listeners», and the «quantity of TV viewers» are used. These do not entirely reflect the economic factors of the intellectual sphere.

Problem II. The «stream of visitors» acts as a «labor subject» in terms of political economy. It should be placed next to the other economic resources participating in the creation of intellectual services. However, the «stream of visitors» has not been evaluated economically and hence not included into the cost of intellectual services.

Problem III. The time factor has been insufficiently used in the theory of the intellectual sphere. It is not considered along with the «stream of visitors», though it would have enabled us to understand what is going on in the intellectual sphere.

Problem IV. The economic theory of the intellectual sphere has not acquired its own economic terminology. Different languages are used here.

Indeed, the analysis of economic literature on the problems of the intellectual sphere shows that many categories, conceptions that are used here have become obsolete, and do not correspond to present day demands. A «viewer» and a «visitor» act as estimation indicators. They have not changed since Pifagorus—for 2500 years. Such stability in evaluating intellectual services shows that the economic thought either «moves in a circle» or has reached a deep deadlock from which it can not find the way out.

A lot of things are absent in the theory of the intellectual sphere:

- there is no precise definition of economic elements;
- the structure of economic elements has not been described in a proper way; the peculiarity of economic relations has not been disclosed;
- it is not clear whether there are proportions between intellectual values and intellectual services;
- where is the economic essence of a complex product of the intellectual sphere?

- what is the structure of an economic product of intellectual sphere?

- what are the peculiarities of the movement of a complex economic product?

- how are resources of the intellectual sphere used?

- what economic criteria should be applied here?

- what should be the target indicators of intellectual welfare?

Clear contours of definitions—the «intellectual welfare of the population» and the «intellectual prosperity of the population of a country»—are absent in the theory. We are in the situation when we do not know what is in an «intellectual consumer basket».

Besides this, there are no methods of calculating the indicators of the intellectual welfare of the population.

The «intellectual welfare of the population» should be logically connected with the expenses spent by a society to achieve a definite level of the intellectual prosperity.

But all these key elements are not given in the economic theory of intellectual sphere. Thus, even from the first lines of this book, the reader sees that basic economic categories described in the economic theory are not sufficiently precise. Economic aims are not determined.

The time has come to work up an economic language (Esperanto) for the intellectual sphere, a language which will be understandable to everyone.

## COORDINATES OF THE INTELLECTUAL SPHERE

Every nation has to be aware of the coordinates of development in the intellectual sphere of the country.

If you go to a large public library intending to acquaint yourself with the economic problems of the Intellectual sphere you will find one or two publications on the subject per, maybe, a thousand volumes on the economy of material production. You will fail, however, to discover books entitled e.g.:

Economy of schools;
   Economy of colleges;
   Economy of universities; **Educational branches**
   Economy of library;
   Economy of exhibitions;
   Economy of museums;

Economy of concerts;
Economy of theatres; **Enlightenment branches**
Economy of circuses;
Economy of Churches;
Economy of cinemas;
Economy of entertainment (attractions, aqua parks, DisneyLands);
Economy of entertainment (summer sports);
Economy of entertainment (winter sports);
Economy of football;
Economy of ice-hockey;
Economy of ball-hockey;
Economy of field hockey;
Economy of basketball; **Entertainment branches**
Economy of volley-ball;
Economy of baseball;
Economy of rugby;
Economy of «Formula - 1»;
Economy of Radios;
Economy of TV.

The absence of these signifies that the economic theory lacks a vast layer of knowledge. For this reason the participation of the above branches of economy in the social production has likely been pushed back from the foreground to the rear. They are regarded as having minor, or secondary, importance.

We cannot speak definitely about the economic coordinates of the intellectual sphere, what is placed on axis «X», on axis «Y», etc. We do not know the aggregate vector of its development or even the direction of its movement.

There are a number of problems which have to be solved now.

It has become a common point that «Education», «Enlightenment» and «Entertainment» branches create intellectual food. They form the «intellectual consumption basket» of the population.

It is not an easy task to establish the economic vector of their movement. There are multiple problems here which have not been solved theoretically yet. For instance, how do we establish the vectors of development of 25 intellectual sphere branches? Each of the branches has its own «internal qualities». Different factors influence the vector of movement. We can speak of legal, economic religious factors and relations here. They exist in different planes. Using a graphic interpretation of social relations they may be shown as follows:

Where
a1—legal relations
b1i—economic relations
C1j—religious relations

$$Z1 = a1 + b1i + C1j$$

The development vector of the intellectual branches differ from country to country. That is why they should be classified and arranged in their respective places.

It is also important to find out how the legal, economic and religious components affect the aggregate vector of the intellectual sphere development: does it subdue, accelerate or refine it?

We shall avoid stereotypes, patterns, etc. and have not only one or two but a series of estimates for every variant of classification:

- estimates of a legal character (a1, a2, a3 ... );
- estimates of a economic character (b1i, b2i, b3i ... );
- estimates of a religion character (C1j, C2j, C3j ... );

The vector of social relations for each of the branches can be shown as follows:

R1 = a1 + b1i + C1j—vector of the development of schools
R2 = a2 + b2i + C2j—vector of the development of colleges
R3 = a3 + b3i + C3j—vector of the development of universities
R4 = a4 + b4i + C4j—vector of the development of libraries
R5 = a5 + b5i + C5j—vector of the development of exhibitions
R6 = a6 + b6i + C6j—vector of the development of museums
R7 = a7 + b7i + C7j—vector of the development of concerts
R8 = a8 + b8i + C8j—vector of the development of theatres
R9 = a9 + b9i + C9j—vector of the development of circuses
R10 = a10 + b10i + C10j—vector of the development of churches
R11 = a11 + b11i + C11j—vector of the development of cinemas
R12 = a12 + b12i + C12j—vector of the development of the services of
sports-entertainment characters (attractions, aqua parks, DisneyLands)
R13 = a13 + b13i + C13j—vector of the development of the services of
entertainment character (summer sports)

$R14 = a14 + b14i + C14j$—vector of the development of services of an entertainment character (winter sports)

$R15 = a15 + b15i + C15j$—vector of the development of football

$R16 = a16 + b16i + C16j$—vector of the development of ice-hockey

$R17 = a17 + b17i + C17j$—vector of the development of ball-hockey

$R18 = a18 + b18i + C18j$—vector of the development of field hockey

$R19 = a19 + b19i + C19j$—vector of the development of basketball

$R20 = a20 + b20i + C20j$—vector of the development of volley-ball

$R21 = a21 + b21i + C21j$—vector of the development of baseball

$R22 = a22 + b22i + C22j$—vector of the development of rugby

$R23 = a23 + b23i + C23j$—vector of the development of «Formula -1»

$R24 = a24 + b24i + C24j$—vector of the development of Radios

$R25 = a25 + b25i + C25j$—vector of the development of TV

The vector of their development depends on the quality of legal and economic relations:
1. Under the conditions of private ownership of the means of creating intellectual services, the development vector of the above branches have one direction.
2. Under the conditions of public ownership of the means of intellectual services, the development vectors of the above branches have another direction.
3. The vector of the development of these branches will be changing depending on the religion component.

In Orthodox countries the development vectors of all the branches will have certain directions; in Catholic nations they will be different.

Proceeding from this, we can draw a special Table of the development vectors of the intellectual sphere branches. Each of the squares (or cells) of the Table will comprise the ordinal number with some other economic parameters. Such a system of evaluation will allow us to properly arrange everything in places according to some of the logical criteria.

## ABOUT COMPLEX NUMBERS

Today complex numbers have been extensively used by researchers:

- in formalizing physical processes of elaboration of composite materials as well as in developing programme products UDF in SQL Server 2000 (Microsoft).

The parties to these developments do not confine themselves to the framework of real numbers. They proceed further. They experiment using complex numbers in their research.

However, it is necessary to point out that regarding the economic theory complex numbers do not find proper application, i.e. economic processes are being examined without using them.

For the time being categories, relations, estimates and criteria of the economic theory have not been classified into series and tables. They are chaotically piled up as an exotic medley.

First of all, by emphasizing that complex numbers should indeed be widely used in economy related sciences, since they would be helpful in systematizing economic relations, estimates, criteria and indicators.

Graphically, a complex number can be represented as follows:

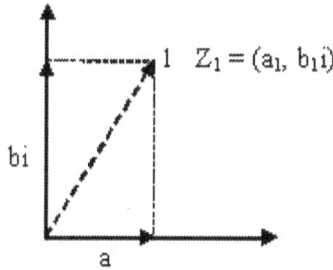

where,
    a1—Real numbers
    b1—Imaginary numbers

$$Z1 = a1 + b1i$$

Complex numbers with two imaginary components may be shown in a three-dimensional space as:

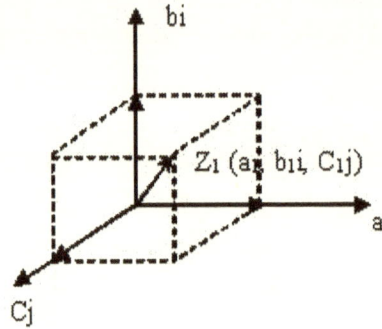

where,

Cj—imaginary numbers;

i, j—imaginary units reflecting the different nature of the origin of the product;

$Z1 = a1 + b1i + C1j$

It is necessary to implement the operational system applicable to a complex number:

a) addition of complex numbers;

$$z_1 + z_2 = (a_1 + b_1i) + (a_2 + b_2i) = (a_1 + a_2) + (b_1i + b_2i)$$

b) subtraction of complex numbers;

$$z_1 - z_2 = (a_1 + b_1i) - (a_2 + b_2i) = (a_1 - a_2) + (b_1i - b_2i)$$

c) multiplication of complex numbers;

$$z_1z_2 = (a_1 + b_1i) \times (a_2 + b_2i) = a_1a_2 + a_1b_2i + a_2b_1i + b_1b_2i^2 = a_1a_2 + a_1b_2i + \\ + a_2b_1i - b_1b_2 = (a_1a_2 - b_1b_2) + (a_1b_2 + a_2b_1)i$$

d) division of complex numbers.

$$\frac{z_1}{z_2} = \frac{a_1 a_2 + b_1 b_2}{a_2^2 + b_2^2} + \frac{(a_2 b_1 - a_1 b_2)i}{a_2^2 + b_2^2}$$

Format: Paperback
Size: 6 x 9
Pages: 270
ISBN: 9963-633-45-5
Published: November 2003

978-0-595-44127-3
0-595-44127-0

www.ingramcontent.com/pod-product-compliance
Lightning Source LLC
Chambersburg PA
CBHW030934180526
45163CB00002B/558